CREATING
AND
PRODUCING
THE
PERFECT
NEWSLETTER

Scott, Foresman Business Writing Series

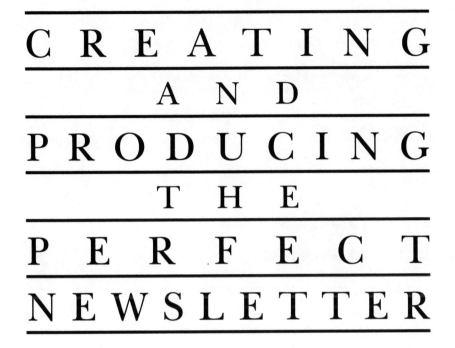

CREATING AND PRODUCING THE PERFECT NEWSLETTER

Patricia A. Williams

SCOTT, FORESMAN AND COMPANY

Glenview, Illinois   London

Library of Congress Cataloging-in-Publication Data

Williams, Patricia A.
    Creating and producing the perfect newsletter / Patricia A. Williams.
        p.   cm. — (Scott, Foresman business writing series)
    ISBN 0-673-46004-5
    1. Newsletters—Publishing.   I. Title.   II. Series.
Z286.N46W54   1990
070.1'75—dc20   89-10851
                                                               CIP

1 2 3 4 5 6 KPF 94 93 92 91 90 89

ISBN 0-673-46004-5

Scott, Foresman professional books are available for bulk sales at quantity discounts.
For information, please contact Marketing Manager, Professional Books Group,
Scott, Foresman and Company, 1900 East Lake Avenue, Glenview, IL 60025.

ACKNOWLEDGMENTS AND CREDITS

I would like to thank the following people for their assistance in preparing this book:

Jeremy Robkin of InnoVisions Creative Services, for his generosity in supplying information and materials on desktop publishing and for creating the screens used in several of the figures in this book.

Robert Kildall of Olympic Distributors, Inc., for information and materials on electronic stencil duplicating.

Deborah Batjer of Deborah Batjer & Associates, for information and material on desktop publishing.

Thanks also to Logitech, Inc., for permission to reproduce material from the ScanMan™ User's Manual Addendum.

I also want to thank the following editors and publishers for permission to reprint and reproduce material from their newsletters:

> *basically business* (Fall 1988). Published by Sir Speedy Printing Center, Renton, Washington.

> *The BPM Newswave* (April 1988, Volume II, No. 2), editor Sara Wiebort. Published by Balcor Property Management, Inc.

Northwest DANCE Focus (Volume VIs, No. 3, November 1988), editor Sandra Kurtz. Published by the Northwest Dance Coalition.

Raima Record (Volume 1, Number 1, July–August 1988), editor John V. Hedtke. Raima Corporation, copyright © 1988.

Raytheon News (September 1988), manager of editorial services Kenneth J. Tokarz. Published by the Raytheon Company.

Renton Report (Volume 4, No. 3), editor Charmaine Baker, graphic artist Sylva Coppock. Published by the City of Renton and The Word Works.

Sentinel (September 1988, Volume XXXI, Number 7), managing editor Barbie Falconer. Published by TRW Inc, © 1988.

The Skyliner (Fall 1988 and December 1989), editor Irene M. Dickson. Published by The Norman Company.

The Source (Fall 1988), editor Bill McCuddy. Published by CityFed Mortgage Company.

Update (July 1987 and August 1988). Published by the Laboratory of Pathology, Nordstrom Medical Tower.

From Waldenbooks *60 + Newsletter*, (July/August 1988 and November/December 1988), © copyright writer/editor, Allia Zobel. Published by Waldenbooks, all rights reserved.

The WRQuarterly (Number 6, March 1988, Number 7, June/July 1988, and Number 8, Fall 1988), editor Jill Shriver. Published by Walker Richer & Quinn, Inc. © Copyright 1988.

TRADEMARKS

Apple and Macintosh are registered trademarks licensed to Apple Computer, Inc.

CricketGraph is a registered trademark of Cricket Software.

GEM and Digital Research are registered trademarks and GEM Paint, GEM Graph, GEM Draw Plus, GEM Desktop Publisher, and GEM WordChart are trademarks of Digital Research, Inc.

IBM and PC are registered trademarks of International Business Machines Corp.

Kroy is a registered trademark of Kroy, Inc.

Lanier is a trademark of the Harris Lanier Corporation.

Linotype, Linotron, and Linotronic are registered trademarks of Allied Corp.

LOGITECH, PaintShow Plus, and ScanMan are trademarks of Logitech Inc.

MacWrite is a registered trademark of the Claris Corporation.

Metro ImageBase is a trademark of Metro Creative Graphics.

Microsoft, MS-DOS, and Microsoft Word are registered trademarks of Microsoft Corporation.

PageMaker is a registered trademark of Aldus Corporation.

PostScript is a trademark of Adobe Systems Inc.

Raima, the Raima logo, db_VISTA, db_QUERY, db_REVISE, and db are all trademarks of Raima Corporation.

SuperPaint is a trademark of Silicon Beach Software.

Ventura Publisher is a registered trademark of Ventura Software, Inc.

Wang is a registered trademark of Wang Laboratories, Inc.

WordPerfect is a registered trademark of WordPerfect Corporation.

Xerox is a registered trademark of the Xerox Corporation.

CONTENTS

5

6

7

11

Designing Your Newsletter   193

12

Laying Out and Making Up Pages   243

13

Managing Distribution   277

INTRODUCTION

A *perfect* newsletter may seem an impossible achievement, but it is possible to write and produce a newsletter that's perfect for your organization. Such a newsletter not only serves its readers, it also accomplishes clearly defined goals for the organization and accurately reflects its image.

Creating and Producing the Perfect Newsletter contains step-by-step instructions that take the uncertainty and drudgery out of planning, writing, designing, and producing the perfect newsletter. It will help you create a newsletter—or improve an existing one—and then serve as a reference for both present and future editors and staff members.

I've written, edited, and designed numerous newsletters, and the experience has been both rewarding and enjoyable. In this book, I pass on what I've learned and show you how other newsletter editors and publishers from all over the United States write and produce their newsletters. *Creating and Producing the Perfect Newsletter* answers the following questions:

○ What types of stories should you feature?

○ Where do you find the stories and other material for your newsletter?

○ How can you write lively and interesting stories?

○ Can you use photos in the newsletter, and if so, how do you get photos that are good enough to print?

○ How do you choose a design for the newsletter?

○ How do you prepare a newsletter for printing? Should you use the traditional method or desktop publishing? What method of printing is best?

○ How will you distribute the newsletter?

This book also answers a question that some people never think to ask:

○ How do you create and shape a newsletter that will enhance your organization's image and accomplish its goals?

This book reviews several complex topics such as photography, graphic design, typography, desktop publishing, and print production. If you want to read more about any of these topics, see the "Resources" section at the end of this book. It lists helpful books, publications, and organizations.

WRITING YOUR NEWSLETTER

Writing is the subject most likely to be glossed over when people talk about putting a newsletter together. But news and feature stories are what newsletters are all about—the heart of the publication. Like any other discipline, writing has standards and techniques that make the work easier and the results more pleasing. This book tells how to

O choose a writing style

O construct different types of stories and columns

O polish and enliven your writing with time-honored techniques

Examples from a wide range of newsletters illustrate the advice and instruction.

TRADITIONAL AND DESKTOP PUBLISHING METHODS

The chapters on print production contain information on conventional methods as well as the newer ones based on computer technology, such as desktop publishing and other page makeup systems.

These chapters review all the options for producing type and art and for making up pages. You'll find step-by-step instructions for making up pages the traditional way—on paste-up boards—and the new way—on the computer screen. You can see how a page of Linotronic output looks compared to typeset galleys, and what a desktop publishing "paste-up" looks like as it's being composed on the computer screen.

ENHANCING YOUR ORGANIZATION'S IMAGE

Throughout this book, with all its explanations, instructions, and examples, there's a strong emphasis on image. Your organization's image may be casual, jolly, and laid-back. Or reserved, polished, and dignified. Or brassy, fun, and colorful. Whatever the image, this book shows how to use your newsletter to polish and enhance it.

Creating and Producing the Perfect Newsletter explains how to tailor a newsletter that will fit your image by using:

1. Content. Should the articles focus strictly on business? Or should they mix business and human interest?

2. A name. Should your newsletter's name sound breezy and friendly? Or strong and bold?

3. Writing style. Should the language be casual, informal, and peppy? Or reserved and dignified?

4. Design. Should your newsletter look gay and dashing? Or sober and reliable? Or . . . ?

This book helps you make your newsletter the voice of your organization.

REAL-LIFE EXAMPLES

Creating and Producing the Perfect Newsletter, using examples from actual newsletters, gives step-by-step instructions for planning, writing, taking photographs, and producing a newsletter. The examples are drawn from all kinds of news-letters, ranging from simple one-page newsletters published for a few dozen readers to slick, glossy ones produced by seasoned professionals for a national audience.

Organizations publish newsletters for many reasons—to sell products, to serve the community, to entertain, to improve employee morale—and the newsletters in this book give you an effective cross section.

Publishing a newsletter is a lot of work, but it's also creative, fun, and gratifying. All the newsletter editors I talked with while I was preparing this book mentioned the satisfaction they felt each time they planned an issue of their newsletter, worked hard to bring it to life, and then saw the final results roll off the press or out of the copy machine.

If you are about to step into the world of newsletter publishing, use *Creating and Producing the Perfect Newsletter* in good spirits and remember that a *perfect* newsletter meets the needs of both your readers and your organization. As for actual perfection in every detail, most readers don't expect it or even want it.

CHAPTER 1

Planning and Managing

ESTABLISHING GOALS

IDENTIFYING YOUR READERS

DEFINING YOUR ORGANIZATION'S
IMAGE

CHOOSING A NAME

DECIDING ON CONTENT

LOOKING AT THE PUBLISHING
PROCESS

WORKING WITH DEADLINES

BUDGETING

What's involved in planning a newsletter? First, you establish the goals that you want your newsletter to accomplish. Then, you decide who you want to read it and what kind of image you want to project to those readers. Next, your newsletter has to have a name . . . correction, *the* name, the one-and-only name that captures perfectly the essence of your newsletter. Along with choosing a name, you decide what kind of stories to run. Then, you need an overview of the tasks involved in publishing a newsletter and how to get each issue out on time. Finally, you answer questions about costs. A well-planned newsletter—one with definite goals supported by both design and content—can accomplish a lot for your organization, maybe more than you realize.

Whether you're already publishing a newsletter or trying to get one off the ground, this chapter contains practical information and advice.

ESTABLISHING GOALS

You may have certain goals clearly in mind for your newsletter and know just exactly what you want to accomplish. Perhaps you want customers to know more about all the services your organization offers. Maybe you want to make the people who staff your branch offices feel more like valued members of the team. Or your goals may be vague; you know only that you want a newsletter to help boost annual sales.

Do some brainstorming. Here, to give you a start, is a list of some of the many objectives a newsletter can accomplish for an organization:

○ Make the organization better known and its name more readily recognized.

○ Give the organization a clearly defined image.

○ Give readers a clearer idea of what the organization does.

○ Make readers feel as if they are members of a team.

○ Announce events.

○ Explain policy decisions or changes in procedures or the raising of fees or charges.

○ Educate readers so that they will support legislation or lawmakers favorable to the organization, the industry, or the field.

○ Educate readers so that they can make more informed decisions for the public good.

○ Interpret national or local news that may be confusing or upsetting.

○ Entertain or amuse readers.

○ Inspire readers to support the community, the church, or the public good.

○ Help the organization gain new members.

○ Help the organization keep its present members.

○ Help the organization make bigger sales.

O Help the organization sell more of its services or products.

O Motivate readers to take action, to improve their minds, their health, or their spiritual well-being.

O Inform readers about new developments.

O Report the news.

O Persuade readers to adopt a point of view.

O Improve or maintain morale.

If your organization is relatively small, defining your goals is simple. As an example, let's say you run a bookstore, Folio Books, that is located in a university town and that competes with two other large bookstores. You believe that a newsletter will help develop a loyal clientele for your store so that you can sell more books. The newsletter will promote books, entertain readers, and demonstrate that Folio Books is an important part of the literary community.

Sometimes, however, establishing goals is more complicated, and to reach a major goal, you may have to accomplish three or four smaller objectives along the way. For instance, your organization might be an insurance company with a large main office and branches nationwide. Let's call it SecureCo. The branch offices are so widespread that employees have found it hard to function as a well-integrated team. You hope that a newsletter will improve this situation. Creating a team feeling among all the employees, then, is your primary goal. But you might need to accomplish some secondary goals first. For instance, how *do* you make staff members feel like a team? You might need to

O explain the rationale of company decisions

O interpret local and national news that affects the insurance industry and, therefore, the company and its employees

Now, you need to establish a primary goal or goals for *your* newsletter. Jot down a brief statement, defining the goals in a sentence or two. Then, if you need to, write down several secondary goals that would help you accomplish the primary one. Ask others who may be involved—superiors, associates, newsletter staff, members—for input.

Keep this statement of goals handy. As you get deeper into your plans, you may decide to refine it. Later, you will use the list to help make decisions, such as what type of articles and features to use in the newsletter.

IDENTIFYING YOUR READERS

Once you establish your goals, you should write a *readers' profile*, which identifies and describes your readers. People use newsletters to communicate with a variety of audiences. Here is a sampling:

- customers
- potential customers
- members
- prospective members
- leaders of groups in a common field or a common organization (leaders of youth groups or managers of offices in a company network, for instance)
- employees
- the media—radio, television, newspaper, and other journalists
- staffs of nationwide organizations

Who are *your* readers? Identify each group of readers that you want to reach with your newsletter. After you identify them, new objectives may come to mind. For instance, readers of SecureCo's newsletter include employees at the main office and staff at the branch offices nationwide. At this point, it's clear that one more goal should be added: Make employees at all offices better acquainted with each other.

On the other hand, Folio Books' list of readers doesn't bring any new objectives to light. Their readers will be university students, university teachers, and townspeople who like to read.

Study *your* list of readers and see if you want to add any new goals.

Now, you need an accurate profile of your readers, which will help you zero in on content and on the image your newsletter should project for your organization.

Your organization may be like Folio Books, with a newsletter aimed at readers with one particular interest so that a readers' profile is easy to write. The readers that Folio Books wants to attract are simply people with literary interests.

If your organization is larger, you may have to do a little more analysis. The following questions can help you focus on your readers.

○ What type of work do your readers do?

○ How would you categorize their jobs? Professional? If so, what profession? Technical? Trades? Retail? Creative? Scientific? Fashion? Recreation?

○ Are they in management? Upper management? Midmanagement?

○ Are they beginners in their profession or area of interest? Or are they experienced and accomplished?

○ What is their average annual income?

○ What type of family group are they in? Young singles? Marrieds with no children? Young marrieds with small children? Middle-aged marrieds with teenaged and college-aged children? Retirees?

○ What are their cultural interests? General interest magazines? Popular fiction? Literary novels? Nonfiction books? Television, movies, videos? Theater, ballet, and opera? Art?

○ Does the organization support any activities related to these interests?

○ What sports do they participate in? Boating? Bowling? Swimming? Camping and hiking? Jogging? Skiing? Racket sports? Softball?

○ Does the organization sponsor any of these activities?

○ What other interests might they have? Fitness? Home improvement? Investments? Politics?

○ Does the organization sponsor any activities related to these interests?

○ What is their interest in your organization? A steady job? Profit? The quality and cost of service? The quality and cost of the product? Community involvement?

○ What do you think your readers would like to read about in your organization's newsletter?

The answers to some of these questions may be readily available. If your newsletter is for employees, your personnel department should have helpful information. If your newsletter is for customers, your marketing department may be able to supply you with some of the information you need.

For instance, SecureCo will send its newsletter to its board of directors as well as to its employees. The readers' profiles might read like the following:

READERS' PROFILE, GROUP A

Employees, professional and technical:
    Average annual income—$25,000–$45,000
    Average age—37
    Family status—married with children
    Interests—civic affairs, investments, travel
    Sports—boating
    Focus on organization—welfare of the company and employment

READERS' PROFILE, GROUP B

Employees, support:
    Average annual income—$18,000–$25,000
    Average age—32
    Family status—young, married with children
    Interests—home improvement, recreation
    Sports—company softball team
    Focus on organization—employment

READERS' PROFILE, GROUP C

Board of directors:
    Average annual income—$45,000–$250,000
    Average age—54
    Family status—married, children grown
    Interests—investments, cruises
    Sports—sailing
    Focus on organization—effective service, community involvement

Keep your readers' profile handy along with your definition of the newsletter's goals because both will help you decide on content, writing style, and newsletter design.

DEFINING YOUR ORGANIZATION'S IMAGE

Your organization may already have a clearly defined and carefully nurtured image. Now is the time to put it into words. If you need to establish an image for your organization, here is a list of adjectives to get you started.

friendly	businesslike	upscale
dignified	fun	salt-of-the-earth
elegant	laidback	exclusive
cultured	sporty	elite
folksy	healthy	beautiful
kind	natural	philanthropic
gutsy	bold	colorful
dynamic	competent	helpful
tasteful	funky	youthful
experienced	free-spirited	civic-minded
arty	literary	musical
spiritual	intellectual	scientific
technical	modern	old-fashioned
classical	traditional	sober
refined	innovative	cool

For instance, a bank might choose these words: traditional, sober, dignified, competent. Or, it might decide that it's time to change its image and choose instead: just folks, helpful, competent, old-fashioned.

SecureCo, our insurance company, would probably choose these adjectives: efficient, reliable, down-to-earth. Folio Books, on the other hand, might choose these adjectives: literary, traditional, academic.

To describe *your* organization, choose at least three words but no more than five. Don't limit yourself to the words in the list either. Get some input from the other people involved with the newsletter. You might photocopy this list and ask the others to pick three to five of the adjectives just as you did. If you all choose the same words, you're in business. If you come up with more than five, then you have a new list to work from. Sit down with everyone and go through the new list of adjectives until you can settle on three.

You'll use this word portrait when you make important decisions about your newsletter's style, content, and appearance.

CHOOSING A NAME

What's in a name? In a newsletter, quite a lot. The last time I was involved in selecting a new name, our newsletter's staff held a contest and asked the employees to pick the name. The response was good and we had many wonderful suggestions as well as a few that were completely off the wall. (Could anyone seriously suggest *Wau Wau?*) Finally, we narrowed the field to five and the director of our department picked the winner. That was several years ago and the newsletter, for employees of an insurance company, still carries the same name on its masthead: *Contact*. It seemed perfect then and seems perfect now.

Of course, you want the perfect name for your newsletter—one that neatly and cleverly fits your organization's image. Let's take a look at what other organizations call their newsletters. Many firms use straightforward titles that include the company name, like the following:

St. Francis Hospital Bulletin

Danforth News

University Hotel Review

Others use names that include a word that suggests communication.

The Barthelme Flash	*MicroTimes*
Sinclair Journal	*CBJ Report*

Many companies like alliteration.

GordonGram	*Micro Mail*
Parson's Post	*Fidelity Focus*
Renton Review	*Interlake Intercom*

Other organizations like a play on words.

CheckOut (a grocery store chain)

Currency (Boeing Employees' Credit Union)

Etc. (King County Library System)

To generate ideas, look at other newsletters. Go to the library and ask to see the *National Directory of Newsletters and Reporting Services* (Gale Research Company), the *Newsletter Yearbook Directory* (Newsletter Clearinghouse), or "Internal Publications," volume five of *Working Press of the Nation* (National Research Bureau). These publications contain thousands of names.

While you're looking for ideas, remember your organization's image. Many words having to do with communications have certain connotations. For instance, the word *journal* sounds faintly intellectual, possibly even literary. The word *bulletin* sounds businesslike and efficient. *Advisory* sounds authoritative. *Notes* sounds casual and light.

Here are some common words used in the names of newsletters and the connotations they carry.

FRIENDLY	SERIOUS	CULTURED
notes	times	journal
light	advisory	review
tab	interchange	folio
list	report	
guide	viewpoint	
spotlight		
bulletin		
log		

Of course, when combined with other words, the connotations of these words can change. For instance, Howard Ruff edited a newsletter called *Ruff Times*. The play on words brings the name down to earth.

Come up with three to five possible names and then sit down with the other people involved to make a final decision.

Let's use SecureCo's newsletter as an example. SecureCo, as you may remember, wants a newsletter that will interpret news that affects their industry, explain company decisions, and make widely scattered employees feel like part of a team. When they picked adjectives to describe their company's image they came up with *efficient, reliable,* and *down-to-earth.* Here are some possibilities for consideration:

SecureCo Signpost This name sounds serious but not stuffy and it's alliterative. It has a nice ring to it, but does it suggest solidarity or teamwork?

SecureCo Signal Another alliterative name that has the right connotations. But it doesn't have a pleasing ring.

The Signal This name has a better sound than the previous one and suggests communication.

Interchange This name also has a good sound and suggests communication and mutual interests.

Network Although this name suggests togetherness, it just doesn't sound quite right.

The two most pleasing names, then, are *The Signal* and *Interchange*. Although the sound of the letter *s* is desirable in the name, *Interchange* suggests a mutual exchange of ideas and so *Interchange* it is.

Folio Books, of course, will call their newsletter simply *Folio*.

DECIDING ON CONTENT

Now what about your newsletter's content? Stories and regular features should appeal to your readers, help your organization accomplish its goals, and enhance its image.

In 1981 the International Association of Business Communications, which counts 10,000 editors in its membership, surveyed 45,000 employees of forty businesses in eight industrial categories about what they like to read in a newsletter. Here are the results.

RANK	SUBJECT
1	Organization's plan
2	Personnel policies and practices
3	Productivity improvement
4	Job-related information
5	Job-advancement opportunities
6	Effect of external events on job
7	Organization's competitive position
8	News of other departments
9	How their job fits into the company's organization
10	How the organization uses its profits
11	The organization's stand on current issues
12	The organization's involvement in the community
13	Personnel changes/promotions
14	Financial results
15	Advertising promotions/plans
16	Articles about other employees
17	Personal news such as birthdays and so on

If, like me, you're surprised at how serious-minded those 45,000 employees are, you might want to distribute a flyer asking *your* potential readers which topics they would like to read about. Here's a list of topics, including those listed previously, broken down into categories:

NEWS ABOUT THE ORGANIZATION

- Milestones
- Accomplishments
- Announcements of coming events (blood and charity drives, annual meetings, conferences, annual picnics or holiday events)
- Reports on events

NEWS ABOUT EMPLOYEES OR MEMBERS

O Promotions

O Retirements

O New personnel

O Anniversaries

O Achievements

NEWS ABOUT THE COMMUNITY AT LARGE

O Relevant news about the immediate community

O Relevant national or international news

ARTICLES ABOUT THE ORGANIZATION

O The organization's history

O Department, division, or branch profiles

HUMAN INTEREST FEATURES

O Personal accomplishments

O Awards

O Anniversary announcements

O Personality profiles

REGULAR FEATURES

O A column representing the policy-making voice of the organization

O A column with rotating or guest writers

O A gossip column

O Calendar of coming events

O Changes (promotions, new employees, retirements, etc.)

O Classified advertising

When you poll your readers, let them choose from these topics, plus any others that you think might fit *your* readership. You can also give them the option of adding topics that aren't on the list.

If the newsletter is for company employees, polling the readers is easy. You can deliver questionnaires through the interoffice mail, place piles of them in strategic locations, or choose a person in each department to distribute them.

If your readers include customers or scattered members of an organization, you could stuff questionnaires into the envelopes that carry their monthly statements or the packages that contain the merchandise they order. Or if your potential readers meet regularly, hand out the questionnaires at meetings. If a large number of your readers pass through your place of business, place a pile of questionnaires on a table near the entrance. Be sure to put a highly visible sign close by to draw their attention. Another possibility is to ask employees to hand out the questionnaires as they wait on customers.

To give you an idea of what types of stories and columns other newsletters run, you'll find the contents for a variety of newsletters listed in the following paragraphs. From these lists, you can get a pretty clear picture of the goals of each newsletter.

The Skyliner, a newsletter for the tenants of a large office building, provides useful and helpful information to its readers and makes them feel at home in a busy, urban setting by giving them news about the "neighborhood."

○ Announcement of a pumpkin-carving contest being held in a nearby shopping mall.

○ Editor's column reminiscing about concerts attended over the years.

○ Information about the community orchestra's concert schedule.

○ Transportation news for commuters.

○ Calendar of activities in a nearby shopping mall.

○ Announcement of a group tour of a winery.

○ Announcement of exercise classes.

○ Manager's column introducing new employees.

Dedication to Care, a newsletter for the employees and patients of a medical center, acquaints readers with the staff to promote a friendly, caring image. It also includes educational information about health care. Patients who read this newsletter should feel more comfortable about coming to the clinic.

○ Article about two physicians using laser surgery.

○ A message from the executive director about personnel changes.

○ A personality profile, the "Employee of the Month."

○ Four brief personality profiles introducing physicians new to the center.

○ Article about a nurse celebrating thirty-one years of service.

○ Gossip column announcing births, marriages, wedding anniversaries, and engagements.

MIDAMERICANEWS, a newsletter for members (customers) of a large credit union, informs its readers about its services, educates them about credit and money handling, and tells them about the history of the credit union, reminding them that credit unions exist to serve their members.

○ Article about home equity loans, explaining interest rates and tax advantages.

○ Article about opening of a new branch office.

○ Article with advice on credit contracts.

○ Tips for using the automated information system.

○ Chairman's column about credit union's history and growth.

○ Chart showing current interest rates on certificates.

○ Article announcing current loan rates.

○ Brief article reminding readers of credit union's travel agency service.

Folio, our bookstore's newsletter, will carry the following types of stories and features for its book-loving readership:

○ Book reviews.

○ Announcements of visiting authors.

○ News about the literary activities at the university.

○ Articles about local writers.

○ A poetry corner, featuring local poets.

Our insurance company's newsletter, *Interchange*, will carry:

○ News about employees, promotions, awards, and so on.

○ Human interest features, such as personality profiles, and articles about employee accomplishments and interests.

○ News about the company's softball team.

○ News about the community that's relevant to the organization.

○ Articles about the organization, such as its accomplishments and its history, and profiles of branch offices.

○ A column, written in rotation, by the managers of the branches.

Here are a few words of warning about choosing content. If your goal is to increase business or sales, avoid the hard sell. Provide service-type articles and give readers information they need to help them make intelligent choices. If you're selling electronic equipment, for instance, tell readers about innovations and about your products, but also tell them how to take care of the equipment they buy.

If your goal is to increase employee productivity, avoid manipulation and motivational-type articles. What you want to avoid at all costs is a paternalistic stance: the wise, all-knowing benefactor guiding the foolish or wayward employees so that they'll keep their noses to the grindstone. Give employees useful information instead; acquaint them with the company, tell them what's going on, and inform them about the company's plans.

LOOKING AT THE PUBLISHING PROCESS

Publishing a newsletter is creative, fun, gratifying, and a lot of work. Now, we get to the work part.

A newsletter may be a simple one-page affair, typed on the office typewriter, illustrated with one or two pieces of clip art, and copied on the office photocopy machine. Or, it may be a sixteen-page, glossy, full-color production. The basic steps in the publishing process are pretty much the same, however, even though their number and complexity may vary. Here are the steps typically taken in publishing a single issue of a newsletter, beginning with the planning conference and ending with the newsletter in the hands of the happy readers.

1. Plan the issue, including articles, art, and photos.

2. Collect information, interview sources, and take photographs.

3. Write stories.

4. Turn the text of the stories into type.

5. Create or assemble graphic elements including art and photos.

6. Have any necessary photostats, halftones, and photocopies made of the type and graphic elements.

7. Lay out and make a dummy of the newsletter.

8. Proofread type and art, and adjust layout.

9. Assemble type and art to make up the pages for printing.

10. Print the newsletter.

11. If your newsletter is complex, trim, fold, collate, and assemble pages.

12. Distribute newsletter to readers.

If you mail your newsletter, you also:

1. Insert the newsletter into an envelope for mailing.

2. Label and sort.

3. Affix postage, bundle it, and deliver it to the post office.

WORKING WITH DEADLINES

To accomplish these steps and get each issue of your news-letter out on time, you'll have to work with deadlines. Naturally, you want to cover all of the events that are important to your organization. To make this easier, keep a calendar on which you mark not only holidays, but events like the company Christmas party, the summer picnic, the annual meeting, conventions and trade shows, and charity and blood bank drives. Include all of the events that are important to your organization. If you don't have an exact date for an event, put a note on the calendar to check on that event well in advance of the approximate date. Remember, you need enough time to plan, research, and write the story.

After you've published a few issues of your newsletter, the publishing cycle will assume a life and rhythm of its own. Generally, you can adhere to the following method to establish and meet deadlines.

First, check with the people involved in each step of publication. Starting with the end of the cycle, find out how long it takes to

1. Distribute the newsletter to the readers after it's printed. This includes collating, addressing, stuffing, bundling, and mailing.

2. Print the newsletter. This could be how long it would take to have it either photocopied, mimeographed, or printed.

3. Get the final layout approved.

4. Lay it out and paste it up (including both traditional and computer-based paste-up).

5. Compose the type for the stories.

6. Create the artwork.

7. Get photostats or veloxes made.

8. Get the stories approved.

9. Research and write the stories and take photographs.

10. Plan the content of the issue and have the plan approved.

For example, here's an estimate of the time it would take to complete the different tasks involved. The newsletter is 8½ by 11 inches, printed front and back, uses only clip art, is published once a month at a quick print shop, and is delivered in-house.

TASK	TIME
Planning	1 day
Research and interviews	2 days
Writing	3 days
Approval	1 day
Typesetting	2 days
Paste-up	2 days
Approval	1 day
Printing	3 days
Delivery	½ day

Worked out on a calendar, counting only workdays, and allowing time for the unexpected, the schedule for the December issue might look like this:

Planning	November 16
Research and interviews	November 17
Writing	November 22
Story approval	November 25
Typesetting	November 28
Paste-up	December 2
Paste-up approval	December 7
To printer	December 9
Delivery	December 15

A schedule for a four-page newsletter that includes illustrations and halftones, is published quarterly, and is sent
by mail is a different story. The schedule for this more
complex newsletter might look like this:

Planning	May 2
Research and interviews	May 4
Writing	May 12
Story approval	May 19
Typesetting and production	May 23
Paste-up	June 3
Paste-up approval	June 10
To printer	June 14
To post office	June 28
Delivery	July 1

BUDGETING

Estimating how much the newsletter will cost and creating
a budget for it is another administrative chore. If you're
proposing a newsletter to management, you probably need
to come up with a budget as part of your proposal. In a lot
of cases, however, management sets the budget and then
the staff juggles this budget to produce the newsletter.

You may produce your newsletter completely inhouse
or you may farm out all the work. For the average newsletter, some or all production is done inhouse and the printing
is done outside. The following sections give you some idea
of how to develop your own budget, although they don't
cover all the materials, services, and equipment for every
possible situation, of course.

ANNUAL OPERATING COSTS

The annual operating expenses will fall into the following categories:

1. office
2. editing, reporting, and writing
3. typesetting
4. graphics, including paste-up
5. printing
6. distribution

Figure 1-1 provides a form to use for estimating your annual operating expenses.

	Cost per issue	Number of issues annually	Annual cost
Office	$_____.___	× _____ =	$_____.___
Editing, reporting, and writing	_____.___	× _____ =	_____.___
Typesetting	_____.___	× _____ =	_____.___
Layout and paste-up	_____.___	× _____ =	_____.___
Printing	_____.___	× _____ =	_____.___
Distribution	_____.___	× _____ =	_____.___
Total			$_____.___

Figure 1-1. Form for Estimating Annual Operating Costs

In each category, you should include the cost of materials, equipment, and personnel. Personnel might include editors, reporters, writers, photographers, artists, and production personnel (i.e., a typesetter, a printer, or a printer's assistant).

Remember, your company probably provides a benefit package and figures total compensation at a figure above the official salary. For instance, a person making $21,000 a year might have a total annual compensation of $32,000. Also, the members of the newsletter staff may not devote full time to the newsletter. In that case you'll have to prorate their compensation.

For the sake of example, let's say that you spend 25 hours a month, or 300 hours a year, editing your monthly newsletter. Your total compensation is—well, since this is an example, let's be generous—$50,000 a year for 2,000 hours of work. Here's how to figure the cost of your time:

$$\$50,000 \div 2,000 \text{ hours} = \$25 \text{ per hour}$$

$$\$25 \text{ per hour} \times 300 \text{ hours} = \$7,500$$

OFFICE.   The expenses involved in maintaining an office or work area also need to be included. These expenses could include items such as:

○ space rental

○ telephone

○ office supplies such as paper, pens, pencils

○ compensation for clerical support

○ messenger service

EDITING, REPORTING, AND WRITING.   The costs to consider in this category include

O   compensation for editors, reporters, and writers

O   automobile expenses

O   travel expenses, such as hotels and meals

O   tape recorders and tapes

TYPESETTING.   The costs of typesetting could include the following:

O   professional typesetting

O   compensation for an inhouse typesetter

O   compensation for a typist or word processor who produces final copy

GRAPHICS.   Graphics costs include the cost of producing illustrations (including photographs) and the cost of creating paste-ups. Such expenses might include

O   compensation for inhouse artists and computer graphics specialists

O   illustrations created by free-lancers

O   layout and paste-up services

O   Imageset page masters

O   materials such as paste-up boards, masking tape, adhesives, white correction fluid, rulers, knives, scissors

O   transfer letters, borders, and screens

- pens and pencils, templates, and other equipment for drawing lines
- burnishing tools, finishing sprays
- photostats and veloxes
- free-lance photography
- photographs purchased from outside services
- film for the camera and the cost of developing it
- computer diskettes
- computer printer ribbons, paper, or ink cartridges
- supplies for inhouse photostat cameras

PRINTING.   The costs of printing may include

- professional printing services
- compensation for inhouse printers
- paper for photocopying, mimeographing, or printing
- costs for collating, assembling, and binding

DISTRIBUTION.   If you use the mail to distribute your newsletter, you must figure in this cost too.

- mailing labels, for either hand addressing or for your computer
- mailing list maintenance
- addressing and mailing services
- postage

STARTUP COSTS

Startup costs can vary widely and depend on many factors, including your method of production and how much of the work you intend to do inhouse. If you're a one-person operation and your organization provides you with an office, a typewriter, and the use of the company photocopy machine, your startup costs are minimal. If, on the other hand, you decide to purchase a full desktop publishing system, your costs can run into the thousands of dollars. (Chapter 7, "Choosing Production Methods," discusses newsletter production.) You can, of course, amortize the cost of equipment, including major purchases such as a computer or a laser printer.

The items in Figure 1-2 will give you an idea of some of the development costs you might need to consider.

Initial design	$_____.___
Electric typewriter	_____.___
Drafting or light table	_____.___
Waxer	_____.___
Artist's equipment	_____.___
35 mm camera and accessories	_____.___
Computer	_____.___
Computer printer	_____.___
Scanner	_____.___
Other computer hardware	_____.___
Computer software	_____.___
Typesetting equipment	_____.___
Printing press	_____.___
Photostat camera	_____.___
Photocopier	_____.___
Electronic stencil equipment	_____.___
Other	_____.___
Total	$_____.___

Figure 1-2. Form for Estimating Startup Costs

SUMMARY

The right planning and managing techniques can make writing and producing a newsletter much easier. Here is a summary of the important points in this chapter:

1. Establish goals for your newsletter.

2. Identify your readers and write a profile of them so you'll know how to hold their interest with your newsletter.

3. Define your organization's image so that design, content, and language will accurately reflect it.

4. Choose a name for your newsletter that is apt and that carries the proper connotations.

5. Decide what type of articles and stories will serve the readers and help the organization reach its goals.

6. Research production methods so that you'll know how to make a schedule and budget for your newsletter.

Chapter 2 describes how to gather news and conduct interviews and gives information on copyrights.

Gathering News

It's never happened to me, of course, but I've heard horror stories. The deadline is approaching and you can only fill up three pages of a four-page newsletter. What do you do? Print cartoons and jokes? Dig through the clip art books?

This chapter discusses a method for ensuring a steady flow of news and material for your newsletter and explores that vital process of news gathering called the interview. When you know how to conduct an interview, it can be the source of compelling and vital stories and one of the highlights of your job.

As part of news gathering, you may occasionally want to reprint someone else's material in your newsletter. The section at the end of this chapter provides an overview of copyrights.

GATHERING NEWS AND STORY IDEAS

Stories are the grist for your mill. You must have a steady and reliable way to collect ideas, news items, and other material. If you're lucky, you have reporters on your staff to follow up leads, gather information, and conduct interviews. If you're extremely lucky, you get to have all the fun yourself. Irene Dickson, editor of one of the newsletters used in this book, says that although filling the space can be a challenge in some issues, *The Skyliner* is a joy to put together and that people send her more and more news items all the time.

Irene and other newsletter editors employ many devices to collect news. Here are a few you can use to fill the columns of your newsletter.

- O Staff reporters who actively seek stories.

- O *Stringers* (free-lance reporters who cover a limited area for a publication) who may be employees you draft into service.

- O Press releases from publications in the field (write and ask them to put you on their mailing list).

- O Meetings of associations where speeches are made and information is handed out.

- O Publications—newsletters, newspapers, and magazines—that carry news that might interest your readers. (See the copyrights section later in this chapter.)

- O A clipping service. In some fields, a central office will supply material to member organizations for just this purpose.

- O Requests for contributions posted on bulletin boards or in other prominent places.

- O Regular columnists, such as a company official willing to contribute a column.

- O The company library. It probably has historical or biographical documents that you could use.

WORKING WITH STRINGERS

If you work for a large company, you might ask each division or department head to name a person to act as a stringer—someone who will report news and story ideas for their area. You can either use the information as is or investigate it more fully. In some instances, your stringers may write the stories.

To get complete information from stringers or volunteers, give them some guidelines, as in the following example created for a fictional newsletter, *Random Harvest*:

GUIDELINES FOR REPORTING NEWS FOR RANDOM HARVEST

○ Gather as many facts as possible about the story.

○ If you can't verify a fact, circle it and mark it with a question mark.

○ Write everything out in full. We need full names and titles, days of the week along with dates, and addresses along with place names.

○ Write down the names of your contacts, the people who gave you the information. Include their phone number.

○ If you can get photographs or illustrations, send those along too.

○ Write down the names of other people who might have more information, photographs, illustrations, or material for a related story.

○ Send the story in before noon on Tuesday. If you are still checking on some of the facts, call me at 522-1789, and let me know what you have.

When stringers, or other occasional contributors who aren't professional writers, write stories for publication in your newsletter, you should provide editorial guidance. You can ask them to read the sections on writing in this book or, at the very least, give them some tips, as in the following example:

GUIDELINES FOR WRITING STORIES IN <u>RANDOM HARVEST</u>

○ Write a lead paragraph that tells who, what, when, where, why, and how.

○ Write short paragraphs.

○ Put the most important information first.

○ Use action verbs.

○ Use concrete and specific descriptions.

○ If you can't verify a fact, circle it and mark it with a question mark.

○ Write everything out in full, including names and titles, days of the week along with dates, and addresses along with place names.

○ If you can get photographs or illustrations, send those along too.

Use discretion in editing stories submitted by volunteers. Take care of spelling and grammatical errors. Add or delete some commas or edit the stories to fit the space available but think carefully before you do a major rewrite. You may lose not only an important source of material, your stringer, because of hurt feelings, you may also lose that intangible something called personality. Often, the very heart of a newsletter can be in the spontaneous and imperfect articles submitted by volunteer reporters/writers.

DEVELOPING CONTACTS

You can also develop contacts at organizations that generate news in your particular field. For instance, if you work for a large building and development company, you would make contacts with people at city hall and in state legislative committees, the local union, and watchdog groups—all possible sources of news that would interest your readers. Attend meetings, ask influential people in your organization for names, develop a list of contacts, including their phone numbers, and then contact them regularly.

ASKING READERS TO CONTRIBUTE NEWS

You can also ask your readers to send in news stories. Here is an example of such a request.

DO YOU HAVE A STORY FOR RANDOM HARVEST?

Call us at 631-8901 if:

> You have an unusual hobby or know someone else who does.
>
> Your department has achieved a remarkable goal that you think our readers should know about.
>
> You have discovered some new ways to increase productivity that might help others in the company.
>
> You have ideas for any other stories that might interest our readers.

INTERVIEWING PEOPLE

Interviewing is a skill, and it is well worth developing. More than any other source, people have the information that you need, and learning how to ask the right questions and how to listen will make your newsletter informative and vigorous.

You might need to interview, for example, experts and officials outside your organization, experts and officials in your organization, and employees with accomplishments or hobbies that your readers might find interesting.

PREPARING FOR THE INTERVIEW

An interviewer who is well prepared gets the best results from an interview. To prepare for an interview:

○ Make an appointment with the person, explaining what you want to do and how much time the interview will take.

○ If the person doesn't work for your organization, ask to meet in a neutral place such as a restaurant.

○ Ask the person for a photo or, if one is not available, if you can take one during the interview.

○ Ask the person to send you a resume, vita, or press clipping in advance.

○ Prepare a list of the questions you need to ask during the interview.

CONDUCTING THE INTERVIEW

Be considerate by making the subject comfortable and conducting the interview in an efficient manner that doesn't waste time. To conduct the interview:

○ Make sure you have a pen or pencil and paper to record your notes. (I have known reporters who have had to borrow pen and paper from their subjects!) If you feel more comfortable with a tape recorder, use it. But first make sure that it's all right with your subject.

○ Set the ground rules, confirming again how long the interview will take and what it will cover. If there are areas of information that could be sensitive, find out if the person is willing to talk about them.

○ Keep the interview on track without being inflexible. Remember that you have questions that you need answered.

○ Get the facts and check on the details. Get the full name and title of anyone quoted, and the correct title and date of any written material referred to.

○ Be sensitive to the person's mood. Facial expressions, posture, and gestures can give you clues as to what direction you should take.

○ Find out how to contact the person to confirm any details before the article appears in print.

○ Be sure to express your appreciation for the person's time and assistance.

MAKING SURE INFORMATION IS ACCURATE

You've still got some work to do, even after you've said good-bye and thanked your subject. To make sure your information is accurate, write or expand your notes immediately while the information is still fresh in your mind. If you're uncertain about any details, contact the person to clarify them.

In writing news stories, your facts must be accurate. Double-check everything. Some sources of information may be unimpeachable. For instance, when the chief executive officer directs you to announce record earnings for the quarter, you have no problem. But information from more problematic sources must be double-checked. For instance, if Joe Jones in purchasing tells you that the company is moving its headquarters across town, you will of course check with other reliable informants before you rush into print with this news.

Double-check the spelling of names and places and the accuracy of numbers. Ask the person in question. If that isn't possible, call personnel departments or secretaries and look in company directories, city directories, association directories, and telephone books.

When you're checking a fact over the telephone, ask the question twice, rephrasing it each time. When someone spells something for you over the telephone, use a verification system such as A for Able, B for Baker, and so on.

Checking facts is a pretty straightforward task for most stories. However, for the personality profile, it can be less so. Unless you're writing about a public figure whose history is a matter of record, you must depend on your subject's honesty in reporting details.

Generally, this is no problem. Only once have I printed a story that contained information that was not accurate. And when I say *not accurate*, I mean I wrote and printed a story that was a total fabrication.

Someone mentioned to me that a young woman in our organization was also working on a degree at the university at night. Sensing a story, I immediately contacted this young woman, whom I'll call Sally. Yes, Sally told me, she was going to school at night to get a master's in history to go along with her master's in English. She also volunteered the information that she had had a story published in a prestigious literary journal. She mentioned other accomplishments, dating from high school and college, and I duly recorded them. Sally's story was in our very next issue as our personality profile.

The issue hadn't been out too long when reports began trickling in. As it turned out, Sally had an emotional problem; she exaggerated her accomplishments. In fact, she greatly exaggerated them as I discovered. Not too long after the story ran, Sally resigned.

How could I have prevented this? I could have checked with the personnel department to verify that she did indeed have a master's degree in English. She did not. But the idea that this young woman wasn't telling the truth never occurred to me.

The moral of this story is that although it's possible that a subject will lie to you, it's highly unlikely. When you write personality profiles, you must depend on the good will and honesty of your subject.

WORKING WITH COPYRIGHTS

When you reprint information that has been printed in other publications, you must be careful not to infringe on copyrights. In addition, you may want to protect the material in *your* newsletter by copyrighting it. Let's first examine how copyright laws work.

WHAT A COPYRIGHT COVERS

A copyright gives an author the exclusive right to material that she or he has written. Anyone else who wants to use the material must ask the author for permission. The copyright covers only the material itself—such as a newsletter, a book, or a poem—not the idea behind the material. A copyright can protect prose, art, and photographs. It covers the right to

- ○ reproduce the material in any way, such as by photocopying or photostating
- ○ distribute (publish) copies to the public
- ○ derive other works from the material, such as a movie from a play, or a play from a novel
- ○ perform the material, such as a song or a play
- ○ display the material, such as a painting or a photograph

A copyright can be owned by an individual or by an organization.

THE TERM OF A COPYRIGHT

The Copyright Law of 1976 took effect in 1978, and rules are different for material published after that date. Presently, the copyright owned by an individual for material published in 1978 and after lasts that person's lifetime, plus fifty years after the person dies. A copyright owned by an organization lasts seventy-five years after publication of the material.

For material published before 1978, copyrights last only twenty-eight years, with the possibility of one extension for a total of fifty-six years. Anything published before 1906 is in the public domain.

USING MATERIAL FROM OTHER PUBLICATIONS

Anything that is in the public domain, material with a copyright that has expired, and anything printed by the U.S. government may be reprinted. However, you should assume that any other printed materials are copyrighted.

The copyright laws contain a *fair use* provision that gives limited rights to use copyrighted material for comment and news reporting. You can use portions of a work as long as the portion represents less than 3 percent of the total. You may, of course, use printed materials as sources of information to write your own stories using your own words. Since you want to slant the material toward your readers, you probably need to rethink and rewrite it anyway.

You cannot quote extensive material verbatim—more than 3 percent—without getting permission from the copyright owner.

Copyrighted material usually bears a notice such as:

Copyright © 1984 Sentinel Corporation

In a newsletter or magazine, the copyright notice is usually part of the masthead. In a book, the notice is on the back of the title page. If a specific article, illustration, or photograph is copyrighted, the notice will be in a footnote to the article or in a caption for the illustration or photograph.

To get permission, write a letter to the owner of the copyright, and include the following information:

○ A description of your newsletter.

○ A statement as to whether your organization is nonprofit or a profit-making enterprise.

○ A description of the material you want to use in the newsletter. Include a photocopy of the material so that no misunderstandings will occur.

○ A statement that you'll print any type of credit line that the owner wishes.

You may have to pay a fee to reprint the material, but that is not likely.

COPYRIGHTING YOUR NEWSLETTER

The copyright for the material in the newsletter belongs to your employer, unless you have a written contract specifying that the copyright for material you create belongs to you.

The copyright laws are complex. If you want to be sure that your newsletter is copyrighted, put a copyright notice in your masthead. If you don't put this notice in each issue, the material that appears without the notice won't be protected. The law states that the material is protected even if it appears without notice, but there are several stipulations that make it impractical for newsletters.

If you want to prove the exact date of the copyright and if you might want to sue for infringement, you can officially register your copyright. To register your copyright, request file forms (Form TX) from the Information and Publications Section, Copyright Office, Library of Congress, Washington, D.C. 20559. The Copyright Office will send you information about fees, how to fill out the form, and what to send with it.

SUMMARY

Developing methods for news gathering and knowing how to conduct interviews will ensure a steady supply of stories for your newsletter. Here is a summary of the important points of this chapter:

1. Develop a variety of resources for stories, including reporters, stringers, press releases, literature from meetings, other publications, clipping services, contributors, and libraries.

2. Provide guidelines to help reporters and stringers gather information.

3. Prepare for interviews by knowing what questions to ask.

4. Make sure all your information is accurate before printing it.

5. Get permission from the owners of any copyrighted material.

Chapter 3 describes how to choose a writing style suitable for your newsletter and how to set a tone that will appeal to your readers.

CHAPTER **3**

Choosing a Suitable Writing Style

Writing styles vary from publication to publication and you, of course, want to use the style that will speak most clearly to your readers. This chapter first describes the writing styles most commonly used in newsletters. It also discusses how to control the tone of your language by choosing words that reflect your attitude toward the readers.

CHOOSING A WRITING STYLE

You can use any one of these three writing styles—personal, telegraphic, or semiformal—to reach your readers.

THE PERSONAL STYLE

The personal style of writing, which is casual, friendly, and chatty, is appropriate for a newsletter in several circumstances. If your organization is small or if your readers are acquainted with one other, this style may suit your newsletter perfectly. You might also choose the personal style if your organization is located in a small town where readers, if not acquainted with one another, still feel like neighbors.

The nature of your organization could also make a personal style appropriate. If you sell products or services for home or recreation, you might consider the informal, chatty writing used in this style. For instance, if you create and sell country-style decor or sell products or services for children, you want a style that is personal and unhurried, not one that is businesslike, brisk, and efficient.

The personal style might also be appropriate for an organization that has an unstructured or creative management style. In this type of company, you won't see the buttoned-down look; employees wear informal clothing. Power isn't solely the prerogative of upper management in these organizations. Many decisions are made by teams and creative thinking is highly valued.

If you want to use a personal writing style in your newsletter, here's how to create it:

O Address the readers as if they're friends.

O Keep your sentences fairly short and simple.

O Use a sentence fragment every once in a while.

O Make references to shared knowledge.

O Use slang occasionally.

O Use, sparingly, interjections of personal feeling (Whew! Hallelujah!).

O Use a lot of contractions, like *can't, I've,* and *don't.*

The following extract is from *The Skyliner*, a newsletter published quarterly for tenants of a modern office building in an affluent suburb. All the tenants and employees who work in the building may not be acquainted with one another, but they are, in the real sense of the word, neighbors. In this example, note the contractions, the way the writer personally addresses the audience, and the reference to shared knowledge ("Husky fans can relax. . . .").

THE WASHINGTON STATE WINE TOUR

Northwest Corporate Travel invites you to tour the best of the Yakima Valley wine country. This one day tour will depart from the CityFed Skyline Tower on the 15th of October. (Husky fans can relax ... it's been scheduled around this season's games.) As you enjoy the sampling of Washington's finest wines, you'll also be sampling the incredible beauty of the valley's Autumn colors. The tour includes coach transportation, morning coffee and rolls, tours and tasting, lunch at Hogue Cellars, and dinner on the return. The price is $34 per person. You'll leave at 6:45 am and arrive back in Bellevue by 9:30 pm. What a great day.

For additional information, call Northwest Corporate Travel at 455-3212 or stop by Suite 1935 in CityFed Skyline Tower.

THE TELEGRAPHIC STYLE

The telegraphic writing style, which is brief and brisk, is appropriate when your readers are busy people who want only the gist of the news and want it fast. The *Kiplinger Washington Letter* uses this writing style (in fact, the telegraphic writing style is sometimes called the "Kiplinger style").

Here are some guidelines for creating the telegraphic style.

○ Begin each item with a brief topic statement (sometimes called a *sweep line*) instead of a headline.

○ Underline, italicize, or bold the topic statement and any key statements that introduce subsequent topics.

○ Keep paragraphs very short.

○ Use some incomplete sentences.

○ Omit all words that aren't essential to meaning; you don't need subtleties with this style.

If you want to modify the telegraphic style to suit your organization, don't omit the first three guidelines. They are vital in creating this style.

Although the telegraphic style is most often used in subscription-type newsletters, organizations can use it very effectively in their newsletters. The following example is from *Monday Memo*, which is published once a week for busy employees of a medical center.

STEINER TO RETIRE FROM ST. MARY'S
Geraldine Steiner, assistant professor of Nursing, St. Mary of the Plains College, will retire from the Division of Nursing after 40 years. College personnel invite all medical center employees to a reception honoring Mrs. Steiner this Friday, from 2-4 PM in the Faculty Lounge.

MEDIA HELPFUL IN DRUG ADDICTION FIGHT
David L. Trudeau, MD, ATU medical director, is complimenting Melissa Beck of KSNW Television, Channel 3, for her recent five-part series entitled "Teens & Alcohol." He said, "All of us at St. Joseph felt that her series was just one more example of the fine work which is being performed by the Wichita news media to openly discuss the devastating ramifications of alcoholism and drug addiction on today's teenagers." Dr. Trudeau made his comments in a letter directed to the Editorial Page of The Wichita Eagle-Beacon.

The stories in this example are brief, but clear. A word of warning, however: Your goal is to make the stories easy and fast to read. Don't get carried away and omit too many words. I've read newsletters written in this style with sentences so truncated that I had to read them two or three times before I could get the message.

THE SEMIFORMAL STYLE

The semiformal style of writing is probably the most common writing style for newsletters. It should be used when neither the chatty, personal style nor the brisk, telegraphic style is appropriate. To create a semiformal tone in your newsletter:

○ Speak directly to your readers in a conversational tone.

○ Use the personal pronouns *I, we,* and *you.*

○ Use a few contractions, like *can't, I've, don't, isn't,* but not exclusively.

○ Keep most of your sentences short and simple. Mix in some moderately long ones.

○ Use complete sentences.

○ Don't use personal interjections (Geronimo-o-o-o! Yikes!).

○ Don't use references to shared knowledge (other than the field or the trade, of course).

Interchange, our insurance company's newsletter, will use the personal style in one or two stories per issue but the semiformal style in the majority of its stories. The readership is large, widely separated, and composed of three different groups of readers. The use of the personal style throughout would not be appropriate.

Folio will use the semiformal style not only because of its educated and literate readership, but also because its image is traditional and academic.

The following example of the semiformal writing style is from *WRQuarterly,* a newsletter published by a software company for its customers.

REFLECTION ADDS MULTI-SESSION LAT

If you're using DECnet DOS or PCSA, you can now create and maintain multiple LAT sessions with Reflection version 3.0. Switch among existing LAT sessions or even maintain a LAT session while Reflection is not invoked, and utilize memory previously occupied by Reflection. The new LAT support includes commands such as SHOW SESSIONS and SHOW SERVICES to provide information about the host services available. Version 3.0 of Reflection 1 PLUS, 2, 4, and 7 PLUS all have this new multi-session LAT capability.

In addition, Reflection version 3.0 now supports the LIM (Lotus/Intel/Microsoft) 3.0 expanded memory standard and addresses up to 64K of that memory.

132-column support has been added to Reflection version 3.0 for the Paradise EGA 480, Everex EV657, and Genoa video adapter cards.

Interested in an upgrade? Your Reflection master disk and $75 will get you the most current version of Reflection; $50 more to add Reflection's PLUS option, if you aren't currently using PLUS for LAN support or backup and restore capabilities. Call Order Processing for details at (206) 328-6800.

SETTING THE PROPER TONE

Ideally, the tone of the language in your newsletter reflects the attitude of your organization. If your readers are employees, the newsletter can make them feel like respected and necessary members of the team. If your readers are customers, the newsletter can make them feel like welcomed and valued human beings. However, careless use of language can sometimes give readers the wrong impression. Employees can be made to feel like undervalued and overwatched cyphers and customers like statistics on a sales chart.

Readers respond when you show respect for them, use a positive rather than a negative attitude, and use unbiased and nonsexist language.

RESPECTING YOUR READERS

Years ago, I worked for a company as a writer on their monthly newsletter. The content of the newsletter not only seemed designed to brainwash the employees, the tone gave the impression that management saw them as a horde of rebellious adolescents who needed to be shown the right way at regular and frequent intervals. In the following example, I try to recreate an article from their newsletter.

CAFETERIA RULES AND REGULATIONS

The new cafeteria will begin operation Monday, October 1st. ABC Company has installed this facility for the convenience of its employees. In order to keep the cafeteria running smoothly, please memorize the following regulations governing its use:

- ○ Stay in line. Do not attempt to crowd in or have friends save places for you in line.
- ○ Do not leave trays full of dirty dishes on the tables. When you are through eating, return the trays to the counter marked "Dirty Dishes Here."
- ○ Leave the cafeteria immediately after you finish eating. Do not linger in the cafeteria chatting and smoking after you have finished eating.
- ○ Give yourself enough time to eat. Do not enter the cafeteria at 1:55 P.M. expecting a full meal. The cafeteria closes at 2:00 P.M. sharp.

Needless to say, "ABC Company" had a high turnover and low employee morale. Because they were worried about having room to accommodate all of the employees, they created a problem before the cafeteria even opened. What, specifically, makes this announcement sound so patronizing? Admonishments, statements of the obvious, and over-simplified sentence construction conspire to achieve an insulting tone. How could ABC have announced the opening and courteously asked the employees to keep moving?

CAFETERIA OPENS MONDAY!

The new cafeteria, located on the first floor, near the James
Street entrance, opens Monday, October 1st. The hours are
11:00 A.M. to 2:00 P.M. Monday through Friday.

The menus will include soups, salads, sandwiches, a choice of
two hot dishes daily, breads, desserts, and beverages.

As you know, we had to do some creative planning to fit the
cafeteria into the available space, so seating is somewhat
limited. However, the cafeteria should be able to accommodate
everyone if we use it for meals only and do our midday
socializing in the employees lounge.

In the rewrite, the author doesn't mention the obvious;
employees will see the sign telling them where to place the
trays full of dirty dishes. The author also avoids the "we
versus them" tone by including the author (the voice of
management) among those who need to move out of the
cafeteria after eating.

USING A POSITIVE ATTITUDE

Another way to establish the right tone is by writing with a
positive attitude. In general, watch out for negative expressions. You can find them anywhere, but they seem to appear
most often in rules and regulations, directions, and explanations. Here are some examples.

POSITIVE ATTITUDE:

Work in a well-lighted area when applying the
finish.

NEGATIVE ATTITUDE:

When you are applying the finish, don't work in
an area that doesn't have sufficient light.

POSITIVE ATTITUDE:

The project will succeed if we focus our energies on it and give it full priority.

NEGATIVE ATTITUDE:

The project won't succeed if we don't focus our energies on it and give it full priority.

CHOOSING UNBIASED AND NONSEXIST LANGUAGE

You want to write stories that are unbiased and neutral. This means avoiding emotionally colored words, language loaded with innuendo, and stereotypical and sexist language.

BEING NEUTRAL AND OBJECTIVE.   Your story should be accurate in spirit as well as in fact. Take care not to mislead the readers. Give them both sides of the story and any background information that may be necessary to avoid distortion. When you report and interpret, give your readers the facts. Even when you want to persuade readers to your point of view, you'll be more effective if you use facts and logic rather than biased or emotionally colored language.

If you're writing a story in which two factions have opposing points of view, be especially careful to give both sides of the story. Avoid using pejorative labels or terminology that one side has coined to discredit the other side.

Here's an example of a sentence that shows the writer's bias.

ABC Press introduced the latest in a long string of "hot, new authors," Carter Smythe-Jones. Editor G. Bridges deems Smythe-Jones "a fresh voice in the wilderness."

In the lead sentence, the phrase *the latest in a long string* tinges the meaning with skepticism. The choice of the word *deems* in the second sentence is self-conscious, faintly ridiculing the editor's comment. The author's opinion of ABC Press comes through loud and clear. Here is a rewrite:

> G. Bridges, editor at ABC Press, believes that their new author, Carter Smythe-Jones, is "a fresh voice in the wilderness."

In the next example, the use of the word *fragile* implies that the scaffolding was not as sturdy as it should have been.

WORKMAN DIES WHEN SCAFFOLD COLLAPSES

Yesterday morning a fragile scaffolding gave way at the site of the new construction, and a workman plunged three stories to the ground.

This next version eliminates the loaded word, turning the item into an objective and nonjudgmental news report.

WORKMAN DIES WHEN SCAFFOLD COLLAPSES

Yesterday morning a scaffolding gave way at the site of the new construction and a workman plunged three stories to the ground.

AVOIDING STEREOTYPING.   Another way of showing bias is to let stereotyping slip into the story. Most people have had their consciousnesses raised so that they're on the lookout for racial, ethnic, and religious stereotyping, but they may not be quite as sensitive to age, sex, and class stereotyping. You must be especially careful about describing or labeling people unnecessarily. Don't mention the age, race, or religion of a person unless it's pertinent to the story.

Here are some examples of stereotyping, each followed with a rewrite.

STEREOTYPING:

The only witness, George C. Carter, a senior citizen, said that the thief was a young, white male.

WITHOUT STEREOTYPING:

The only witness, George C. Carter, said that the thief was a young, white male.

STEREOTYPING:

Congratulations to Karl Jones and Mary Smith for a successful meeting. Jones led a rousing songfest that began the meeting on a vigorous high note. Next, Smith, with a delicate but sure hand, led the members through the process of creating a job description.

WITHOUT STEREOTYPING:

Congratulations to Karl Jones and Mary Smith for a successful meeting. Jones led a rousing songfest that began the meeting on a high note. Next, Smith, with a sure hand, led the members through the process of creating a job description.

CHOOSING NONSEXIST LANGUAGE. Needless to say, no one in this day and age includes a description of a woman's appearance or clothing in a business-related article or defines her by her status as a wife, mother, or grandmother. For instance, if it wouldn't occur to you to describe the new director of marketing (male) as *a trim grandfather of three*, you surely wouldn't describe the new director of marketing (female) as *a trim grandmother of three*, would you?

Your organization has probably established standards for nonsexist language. But if it hasn't, you can adopt the guidelines in this section.

One way to avoid sexist language is to replace titles and descriptive phrases that are explicitly male or female with generic titles or descriptive phrases.

USE	RATHER THAN
assistant	right-hand man
big job	man-sized job
business person	businessman
chair, or chairperson	chairman
chief, or supervisor	foreman
drafter	draftsman
flight attendant	stewardess
humans, or humankind, or people	Man, or mankind
representative, or service representative	repairman
spokesperson	spokesman
technician, or worker	workman

Another way to avoid sexist language is to use pronouns and adjectives that aren't exclusively male or female. Some writers have tried using he/she and his/her. Others have tried alternating language, using all male pronouns and adjectives in one section and then all female pronouns and adjectives in the next section, and so on. Neither of these solutions is suitable for newsletters. Here are some techniques you can use:

○ Use the plural form rather than the singular.

○ When the noun has to be singular, substitute an article (a, an, the) for a pronoun.

○ Address the readers directly, if it seems appropriate.

The following examples show how to take the sexism out of language.

SEXIST:

Anyone who witnesses a crime should write down his description of the perpetrator immediately.

NONSEXIST:

Any witnesses to a crime should write down their descriptions of the perpetrator immediately.

NONSEXIST:

If you witness a crime, you should write down your description of the perpetrator immediately.

SEXIST:

The new president, to be announced at the annual meeting, will assume his duties in January.

NONSEXIST:

The new president, to be announced at the annual meeting, will assume the responsibilities of the office in January.

SEXIST:

Every secretary should schedule service for her typewriter on a regular basis.

NONSEXIST:

Secretaries should schedule service for their typewriters on a regular basis.

NONSEXIST:

If you use a typewriter, you should schedule service for it on a regular basis.

All of us are guilty occasionally of using words thoughtlessly, but when you're writing or editing your newsletter, exercising a little care can help you avoid offending any of those important readers.

SUMMARY

A suitable writing style and the proper tone will make sure readers understand and enjoy your newsletter. Here is a summary of the important points of this chapter:

1. Use the personal writing style if you want to project a casual, chatty, and informal attitude.

2. Use the telegraphic writing style if your readers need fast and abbreviated information.

3. Use the semiformal writing style if you want to project a straightforward yet friendly attitude.

4. Show respect for your readers by addressing them as intelligent adults.

5. Use a positive rather than a negative attitude.

6. Choose unbiased and nonsexist language.

Chapter 4 gives guidelines for writing news and feature stories.

Writing News Stories and Features

You've interviewed the subject, your notes are in front of you, and you're staring at the proverbial blank sheet of paper. It's time to write the story. If you're reporting on a current happening, you write a straight news story. If you're exploring one aspect of a current happening, or a subject that's not current, you write a feature.

WRITING NEWS STORIES

If your newsletter is typical, news stories—stories about what has happened, what's going to happen, and who will and who has done what—will dominate. To write a good news story, compose a compelling lead and follow it with a body that presents the details in clear and readable fashion.

WRITING A NEWS STORY LEAD

The *lead* (the first one or two sentences that open a story) can be either direct or indirect. Although news stories and features can begin with either type of lead, a news story most commonly begins with a direct lead and a feature with an indirect lead.

THE DIRECT LEAD.   A *direct lead* paragraph contains one or two sentences that tell the topic of the news story. Usually, the topic is clear: *Rose Smith was awarded the Brubaker Award at last month's meeting. A raging fire of unknown origins destroyed Plant I last Tuesday.* Sometimes, however, it may be hard to decide on the focus of the news story. In those cases, ask yourself: What happened? *What* and *who* are usually the topics of a news story. Occasionally, the story focuses on *why* and *how*, but rarely on *where* and *when*.

This example of a direct lead from the *Raytheon News* tells *who* will do *what, when* it will happen, and *where*.

> BOSTON—A coed running team from Raytheon will represent the New England states at the Manufacturers Hanover Corporate Challenge international championship race here on Nov 20.

The next example from *Focus on Technology* tells *who* is doing *what*.

> TSI is pleased to announce the release of an innovative two-dimensional reading program for the VersaBraille II and II+.

Sometimes a direct lead will combine two elements or summarize several, as in this example from *Kent Arts*.

> Conducted by Joseph White, the talented Rainier Symphony will present Brahms' Academic Festival Overture, Piano Concerto No. 1 by Prokofiev, and Franck's Symphony in d minor on Friday, December 16 at 8:00 p.m. at the Kentwood Performing Arts Center.

However, the lead must not contain too much information or it will confuse the readers. The following lead tries to do too much and ends up being muddled.

> Carlton Hotels won the annual Reggie Award for its 1985
> advertising campaign featuring "Carl the Doorman" and
> announced that Joan Richards will become the new director of
> information services on the retirement of the current director,
> Albert Bush.

The writer has to decide which news item is more important, the award or the promotion, and feature that news item in the lead. A better option might be to write two stories.

THE INDIRECT LEAD.   An *indirect lead* (sometimes called a *delayed lead*) is composed of one or two sentences that piqué the reader's curiosity about the subject matter without stating it directly. An indirect lead can consist of an anecdote, a recap of events, or the setting of a scene. Always follow it with a *bridge*, a statement that announces the subject or the theme of the article.

Here's an indirect lead to a news story from *The Skyliner*. The second sentence is the bridge.

> The Bellevue Downtown Association poses the question, "Why
> should the kids have all the fun on Halloween"? Their answer to
> you is to sharpen up your carving knife, rev up your creative
> motor, renew your competitive spirit and enter the "3rd Annual
> Pumpkin Patch" pumpkin carving contest.

You'll find more examples of indirect leads in the features section of this chapter.

WRITING THE BODY FOR A NEWS STORY

The *body* of the news story—the paragraphs that follow the lead—contains details, clarification, documentation, and authority.

Sometimes a news story is extremely brief and is called a short. It consists of a single paragraph or, at the most, one short lead paragraph with a second paragraph documenting the lead. Here, again from *The Skyliner*, is an example.

> Community Transit has just made travel between Snohomish County and downtown Bellevue even easier. In response to rider interest, Community Transit now offers an additional non-stop trip out of Swamp Creek Park and Ride at 7:45 am, arriving at the Bellevue Transit Center at 8:15 am. Additionally, two new return trips out of Bellevue are available at 5:15 pm and 5:42 pm. Arrival times at Swamp Creek Park and Ride are 5:42 pm and 6:17 pm. Schedules reflecting these changes are available at the Bellevue Transit Center and Transit Information Centers located in many building lobbies in downtown Bellevue. Please call the TMA with your questions and suggestions at 453-0644.

To organize the body of a longer story, use one of these methods: inverted pyramid, chronological order, or climactic order. Ordinarily, you'll use climactic order in features rather than news stories.

THE INVERTED PYRAMID.   For most news articles, you'll organize the body in an *inverted pyramid*, so called because information is arranged in descending order of importance. With this organization, readers can get the gist of the story early and stop reading when they have learned all they want to know. There is another advantage. If you run short of space, you can cut the final paragraphs without damage to the story. Figure 4-1 illustrates the concept.

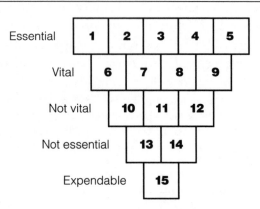

Figure 4-1. A fifteen-paragraph story arranged in an inverted pyramid.

The following example, from *Raytheon News*, is written in a semiformal style and arranged in chronological order. It is a classic example of reporting. The editor could easily cut the last paragraph and, if necessary, end the story at several other points. In fact, the story could run with just the first two paragraphs.

COED TEAM TO REPRESENT NEW ENGLAND IN INTERNATIONAL
ROAD RACE

BOSTON—A coed running team from Raytheon will represent the New England states at the Manufacturers Hanover Corporate Challenge international championship race here on Nov 20.

The team was invited after taking first-place honors at a regional race here in July. The team members are John Clopeck of MSD-Bedford, Steve Sargeant of MSD-Tewksbury, Cathy Carnes of MSD-Andover, and Lauren Heyl of MSD-Tewksbury.

Each team member ran a 3.5-mile course and total times were added for the final results. In winning the regional race, the Raytheon coed team posted a combined time of 73 minutes, 22 seconds.

Coming in second in the coed category was the Bank of New England (76 minutes, 47 seconds). The third-place team was from Digital Equipment Corporation (77 minutes, 20 seconds).

Raytheon entered two other teams in the regional event, which attracted more than 9,000 runners—a men's and a women's team. Teams vary in size for the race. Coed teams have four members, men's teams have five, and women's teams have three.

The men's team finished second with a time of 91 minutes, 11 seconds. Taking first-place honors in the men's category was Digital Equipment Corporation with a time of 85 minutes, 13 seconds.

Raytheon's women's team finished fourth with a time of 70 minutes, 25 seconds. A team from Digital took first place with a time of 61 minutes, 18 seconds. The second- and third-place teams were, respectively, from L. L. Bean and Data General Corporation.

Bob Ward, director of employee motivation programs and running coordinator, said he was "delighted" that the coed team will be representing New England in the corporate championship event. "I feel this is the most competitive group we've ever put together for a national event."

Last year, Raytheon's teams represented New England at the championships in two categories: coed and women's. The women's team finished third and the coed team finished fourth among the international field of runners.

CHRONOLOGICAL ORDER.   Chronological order is the simplest way to arrange the body of a news story. After the lead, simply tell the reader what happened or, as in the following example from *Kent Arts*, what is going to happen. Notice that this story is written in the personal style.

"FOR KIDS FROM ONE TO NINETY-TWO ..."

Mel Torme and Robert Wells' immortal line from The Christmas Song might very well be the only way to describe the holiday festivities the Kent Canterbury Winter Festival will be bringing you this year! Beginning the second annual Canterbury Festival Wednesday, November 30 at 8:00 p.m. in the Kent Senior Center, DUE VOCI will give a free performance of joyous Christmas music from around the world—and in many languages. This outstanding vocal duo claim that being "professional voices" has "never stood in the way of having fun with music" and this is the show to prove it. Like an old-fashioned family gathering, DUE VOCI encourages the audience to join in and sing along with some of these favorite holiday selections.

Saturday, December 3 at 12:00 noon in the Kentwood Performing Arts Center, it's the award-winning TICKLE TUNE TYPHOON in a very special, magical show. Tickle Tune has become a favorite with audiences young and old not just for their energetic music, dance and message of positive self-esteem, but notably for the cast of larger-than-life characters which they always use to touch the imaginations of us all. A holiday show by Tickle Tune can't help but get everyone in the mood of good will—definitely a "don't miss"! Tickets are $5 adults, $3 students/seniors in advance. Tickets are $1 additional at the door. Please call 859-3991 for tickets and information.

On Monday, December 12, at 7:30 p.m., Kent is proud to host a special performance of the Boulding Family/Magical Strings at the Kentwood Performing Arts Center. At holiday time, Pam and Philip Boulding are joined by their five talented children to bring you the unique sounds of Christmas with glorious harmonies, accompanied with celtic harp, hammer dulcimer, violin, cello, and harp, to name just a few!

Magical Strings is just that—magical, and this special holiday show has been internationally acclaimed as the performance "during which you might suddenly feel as if snow is softly falling and you've fallen headfirst into a glorious serene landscape of the pure spirit of Christmas." The Boulding Family concert sold out in Kent last year, so buy tickets early—$5 adults, $3 students/seniors available at Kent Commons and Kent Parks and Recreation. Tickets (if available) will be $1 more at the door. Please call 859-3991 for ticket information.

WRITING FEATURES

Feature stories differ from news stories because the subject may or may not be a current happening and the story explores the subject in depth and in a more leisurely fashion. A feature could be a how-to or service article, giving readers helpful information. The subject matter for feature stories is limitless. Consider topics such as company history; profiles of company departments, divisions, or branches; new technologies; legislation; city, county, or state government; community organizations; and health care.

WRITING A FEATURE STORY LEAD

The lead in a feature story must pull the reader in. Current events have a built-in attraction because readers want to know what is happening, but the subject of a feature may not interest the readers immediately. The lead, along with the headline, has to do more work. For this reason, a feature story usually begins with one of several types of indirect leads. When you have time constraints, however, a direct lead can still do the job.

THE DIRECT LEAD.   You have more flexibility in writing a direct lead for a feature than in writing a direct lead for a news story. For instance, you could begin an article with a question, as the writer did in a story in *Crossroads*.

> Do you know the seven danger signs of cancer?

The lead, although something of a teaser, announces the subject directly.

THE INDIRECT LEAD.   As mentioned earlier, an indirect lead doesn't jump right into the subject matter but piqués the readers' curiosity in some way. An indirect lead can consist of an anecdote, a recap of events, or the setting of a scene. Remember to always use a bridge to link the indirect lead to the body.

In the following excerpt from a story in *Northwest DANCE Focus*, an anecdote leads into the story about a dancer creating a new work. The bridge is the first sentence in the second paragraph.

INSIDE (JESSE JARAMILLO)

I was on my bicycle racing furiously to get to my next scheduled destination when I began down a huge hill. The longer the hill, the steeper it became and the faster I was going. Steeper and steeper and faster and faster, I was travelling on that hill until I went beyond commitment and past the point of no return. Kinesthetically, it was a nose dive and a free fall as my wheels were barely touching the road. I kept saying to myself, "hold on, just hold on." I had felt this sensation as a kid on a swing, I had felt this sensation as my stomach turned inside out on the roller coaster ride at the West Texas Fair. The hill finally curved and banked into level ground as my heart pounded and cold sweat poured down my face. I jerked and sat up in my dark bedroom and for ten seconds was awake in my dream. It was at that time that truth faced me point blank: I was afraid of inner exposure.

Inside Out, exposure, a dance that is felt, not just seen; this was the creative problem I had set for myself.

In the following excerpt from *WRQuarterly,* a recap of events leads into the story about the firm's future marketing plans. The bridge is the third paragraph. Most recap leads won't be as lengthy as this one.

PART 2: HP MARKET STRATEGY

The following is the second in a series of articles intended to inform Reflection users of Walker Richer & Quinn's product plans. The next issue of WRQuarterly will discuss WRQ's Digital market strategy.

Since the introduction of our first communications/terminal emulation product in 1983, Walker Richer & Quinn has supported Hewlett-Packard's datacomm and PC integration strategies. We have dedicated resources to a version of Reflection for the Touchscreen and the Portable Plus, and have supported early Vectra hardware incompatibilities, such as the original multi-mode card. Results from our commitment include an interface to HP's OfficeShare Network and a custom Resource Sharing License agreement for Reflection products. All efforts to date have enhanced the integration of PCs with HP computers and have, in fact, strengthened HP's competitiveness in the mini computer market.

Over the years, a number of new opportunities have presented themselves and demanded our attention. The products resulting from these demands include our Digital VT terminal emulators, terminal emulators for Apple's Macintosh, and support of non-HP LANs. Additional products include an HP 3000-based electronic mail system (PostHaste), a print-sharing utility (RSVP), two PC-to-Email integration packages (DeskDirect and Dispatch), and a PC-to-host cooperative processing tool for developers (PP1). Any or all of these products could be perceived as competitors to offerings from Hewlett-Packard.

However, let me now reiterate—our fundamental HP strategy is to complement and enhance HP's product line and direction.

In the next example, from *Crossroads*, the setting of a scene leads into an article about no-fault insurance. The bridge is the fifth paragraph.

NO-FAULT AUTO INSURANCE (TO BLAME OR NOT TO BLAME?)

It's raining. The roads are miniature rivers, car windows are steamed up and windshield wipers are metronomes hurrying people to their destinations.

Crash. Two cars meet unexpectedly at an intersection in a tangle of metal.

People in both cars are hurt. Two are hospitalized. All, a total of five, have medical bills.

Who pays the medical and repair bills?

Under our present system, the driver guilty of causing the accident is liable, and the companies insuring the other "innocent" parties will try to collect from the guilty party's insurance company. If liability is disputed, a court case may result. Blame is determined. Taking the blame out of auto accidents is what "no-fault" is all about.

The following extract from *Chip & Holly's Newsletter* is an example of an indirect lead that's harder to classify. It has some elements of scene-setting and some of an anecdotal type of lead, but it is also rather startling, like the startling assertion lead you'll read about later. The third sentence is the bridge to the body of the story.

THE BIG PARADE THEN AND NOW

Can you imagine looking up in the sky the day after
Thanksgiving and seeing a humongous hippopotamus float by?
Well if you were around in 1929, you just might have. You see,
back then the people who put on the annual New York City
Macy's Thanksgiving Day Parade decided to end the show with
something spectacular.

THE ROUND-UP (BULLET) LEAD.   The round-up (or bullet) lead shoots nuggets of information at readers and then the bridge ties everything together. You can use the round-up lead in stories about trends or, as in the following example, in stories that uncover the reasons or causes behind certain happenings. The following excerpt from *The Sentinel* fires three barrages at readers and then states the theme of the story in the bridge in the fourth paragraph.

EMPLOYEE INVOLVEMENT: THE KEY TO COMMITMENT,
CONTRIBUTION

Twelve months ago, a spacecraft electronic enclosure box took
about 194 days to produce. Today, O&SG's Manufacturing
Division can whip one up in 104 days—a 46 percent
improvement. And it aims to cut that span to 64 days. The
bottom line will be a 58 percent reduction in costs.

Seven months ago, business as usual turned unusual at TRW
Security Services. That's when teams of employees began
studying different aspects of their job and finding quality
answers to complex questions. DSG's Command Center
Processing Display System—Replacement contract—a large
software development program—claims productivity 20 to 50
percent higher than similar programs.

TRW Components International has more than doubled in size
in two years. From a specialized computer system to new
functional areas, employee input has been an integral part of
TRWCI's rapid evolution.

What's the common thread? Employee involvement (EI)—
where employees have influence in the decision-making process
and a say in how they do their jobs.

THE STARTLING ASSERTION LEAD.   The startling assertion leads the readers into a story in a dramatic fashion with an unexpected or surprising statement. In the following excerpt from a story in *Renton Report*, a community newsletter, the startling assertion is lighthearted. The bridge is the second paragraph.

> FURRY CRITTERS ARE RIDING PATROL WITH RENTON POLICE OFFICERS
>
> There have been recent reports of furry little critters riding patrol with the Renton Police Department.
>   No, they're not the department's German Shepherds, but teddy bears—50 of them—that were donated to the police by Russell Price of State Farm Insurance Company.

WRITING THE BODY IN FEATURE STORIES

When you organize the body of a feature story, you can choose between chronological order, climactic order, or, if space is an issue, the inverted pyramid (see the previous section on writing news stories).

CHRONOLOGICAL ORDER.   Chronological order is effective in writing a history, such as the history of the company or a piece of government legislation or the background of a social movement. One way to approach a department profile is to describe a typical day, using chronological order to follow employees through their tasks.

Chronological order is also effective in informative stories, such as those that explain processes. For instance, you could use chronological order to tell the readers how the new equipment that automates the drafting department works. Or, as in this excerpt from *WRQuarterly*, you could use chronological order to tell readers how to solve a problem.

DEAR TECH SUPPORT . . .

Some Reflection users have host communication problems. Reflection seems to be working correctly (configuration screens can be brought up, characters can be typed in local mode) but nothing happens when you press Return. The problem could be that Reflection is configured for the wrong COM port, the COM port on the PC is burned out, or there's a bad cable connection between the PC and the host. Use a paper clip as a diagnostic tool to troubleshoot your serial port. Here's how:

Rename your AUTOEXEC.BAT and CONFIG.SYS files, then power the PC off and back on again. This insures that no memory resident software is present and that PC hardware is reset. Verify that the COM port is properly installed with the Reflection utility program COMCHECK. Run Reflection from DOS with a default configuration (C:\>R1\D for example). If the troubled serial port is not COM1, configure for the different COM port but don't change anything else.

The description of the procedure continues in chronological order.

CLIMACTIC ORDER.   Another way to organize the body of a feature story is by using climactic order, where you withhold the most important or most dramatic or most surprising information until the end of the story. Because it can be a little tricky and because it loses its effectiveness if it's used too often, this method should be used sparingly.

In the following article from *Dedication to Care*, the information about laser surgery is interesting but the clincher comes at the end.

KMC LASER EXPERTS SHARE SKILL

Only a few OB/GYN physicians in our area are trained in laser surgery and two are on staff at the Kent Medical Center. Both Dr. David Minehan and Dr. Calvin Wallace use the laser equipment at the Green River Surgery Center.

Their laser expertise coupled with a convenient surgery center are the best kept secrets in town.

Many physicians in the area are referring their patients into Seattle for laser surgery. "I had no idea there were physicians in the South end who were trained in using the laser," said Tammy Schunzel, a patient who was referred into Seattle by a local physician for laser surgery to treat severe endometriosis.

As physicians in the area are becoming more familiar with the laser procedure, they are turning to Dr. Wallace and Dr. Minehan for training.

*   *   *

When Tammy Schunzel's gynecologist told her that she would have to go to Swedish Hospital for a laser laparoscopy, she put off the treatment, opting for hormone therapy instead. "I didn't like the idea of going so far away and no one told me there was an option for treatment closer to home," Tammy added.

Later, when her condition worsened, she saw Dr. Parker who recommended she see Dr. Minehan or Dr. Wallace. "I used to work at the Kent Medical Center, so I felt good about seeing a physician there," she added. When Dr. Minehan recommended a laser laparoscopy procedure to treat severe endometriosis, she was surprised to find that Dr. Minehan would be doing the surgery close by at the Green River Surgery Center. "It was great for me," she said. "I wanted a convenient spot so my husband could stay with me."

(Tammy had an extra bonus three months after her laser surgery. She discovered she was pregnant.) "If I hadn't found Dr. Minehan and Dr. Wallace, I would never be where I am today," added a beaming mom-to-be.

SUMMARY

Knowing how to structure your stories makes them more effective and easier to write. Here are the main points covered in this chapter:

1. For most news stories, use a direct lead that gives the topic in one or two sentences.

2. For features and a few selected news stories, use an indirect lead, which may be an anecdote, a recap of events, or the setting of a scene.

3. Always follow an indirect lead with a bridge that explains the topic of the story.

4. Structure your stories using either the inverted pyramid, where you present facts in the order of importance; chronological order; or climactic order, where you withhold a dramatic or surprising fact until the end of the story.

Chapter 5 describes special types of features, the personality profile and the column.

Writing Personality Profiles and Columns

A personality profile is a special kind of feature story that enjoys wide popularity in newsletters. Several types of columns are also very popular. This chapter gives direction for writing these features and the headlines to accompany them or any other story.

WRITING PERSONALITY PROFILES

Personality profiles add warmth to a newsletter; people love to read about other people. They are a bonus for you, too, because they're fun to write. Whether you decide to make them a regular or an occasional feature, you have to answer three important questions:

1. What kinds of information about your subject are suitable as well as interesting?

2. What theme will you use to give the story a focus?

3. What kind of lead will you use?

DECIDING WHAT INFORMATION TO INCLUDE

Generally, the reason you've chosen the person as a subject for a personality profile should determine the kind of information you'll include. In some situations, personal information is not appropriate and you should include only information related to the person's career. If your subject is someone temporarily on the scene for business reasons, like a consultant or a speaker, focus on career information. If you include any personal information at all, limit it to noting the city or community where the person lives and a brief description of his or her family (i.e., name of spouse, number of children).

The subject's status in the organization may also dictate the tone of the story. Generally speaking, the higher the status, the less personal information you include. Exceptions occur when the subject has done something outstanding or unusual outside the organization that's worthy of a feature story. Such a story might focus on a company official's unusual hobby, for instance, or election to an office in the PTA, or successful struggle to overcome personal disaster.

If your organization is very informal or creative, this guideline may not be applicable. But let's face it, personal information is often what people want to read. The formality of your organization, how much the subject wants to reveal, your sense of what is and is not fitting—all of these things can guide you.

Generally, you are safe talking about a person's work history, *current* family situation (a list of marriages and divorces would be in bad taste), and interests or hobbies.

FINDING A FOCUS

A personality profile can be a straightforward rundown on the person, but it will have more punch if you can find a focus. Two very effective techniques for focusing the story are to find a single unifying thread running through the person's life or, conversely, to find a dramatic or surprising contrast. For instance, I once profiled a man, an insurance underwriter, who raced motorcycles on the weekends. The story focused on the contrast between the quiet, methodical work and the dangerous hurly-burly of his hobby.

In another profile, a woman who worked in the cafeteria was not only involved in the organization's annual Christmas-care program, but in several other service-type organizations as well. Her lifetime of involvement with others was the focus of the story.

WRITING THE LEAD

In a personality profile, the lead should alert the readers to the theme or focus of the story. For example, an anecdote can reveal those aspects of the subject that are your focus. A quote from your subject can also make an effective lead.

In the following personality profile, a quote from the subject leads off.

A WOMAN OF ACTION: JUNE SHUMWAY

"There's only so much time," June Shumway says and sighs, because she'd like to have time to do more.

How, you wonder, could she possibly do more? Her involvements are already extensive because June is a practical person who believes in putting her feelings into action. And, she has strong feelings about the value of human beings and their responsibilities to each other.

June, who has worked in the Blue Cross cafeteria since 1966, and her husband Don, are active in behalf of the Rainier School at Buckley and the Millionair Club, a local organization devoted to helping people down on their luck. June emphasizes the last part about people being down on their luck, lest anyone think these people might be bums. She obviously feels that circumstances can alter anyone's destiny.

*   *   *

The Millionairs is just part of what June and Don Shumway find time for. Ask June about Buckley and her eyes soften and she tells you about the little girl they sponsor. "She is so dear to us," she says. Cindy, age 12, is retarded, hyperactive, and has a speech impediment but, June says, "she is very pretty and very loving." For the little girl, the sponsorship means her own spending money, gifts at Christmas and on birthdays, birthday parties and, most of all, people who come to see her, people who care.

*   *   *

Before she came to Blue Cross, June did office work, but that didn't have enough people-to-people contact to keep her happy. She likes her work in the Blue Cross cafeteria and thinks the people are "tops." A native of Shawnee, Oklahoma, her speech is still colored with phrases like "tote," "y'all come," and "tops."

They say that after a certain age, a person's face is of their own making. June's presents a picture of reliability and kindness. As a matter of fact, you can depend on it.

Many people do.

WRITING COLUMNS

A regular column can be a wonderful addition to a newsletter. The most popular columns are written either by a top company official or by rotating columnists. Readers also often enjoy a social or gossip column.

FROM THE TOP

A regular column is a useful tool that management can use to bring important topics to the attention of employees and also to express genuine interest in them. The following column, from the *Raytheon News*, sets just the right tone by reminding employees, in an unpatronizing way, of the value of learning.

MANAGEMENT VIEW
Satisfy Your Curiosity

by Dr. Joseph F. Shea
Senior Vice President-Engineering

Stand still and the world will pass you by.
   Nowhere is that maxim more true than when it comes to education—particularly in the fields of science and technology—but to varying degrees with every discipline or endeavor in life.
   Unless you're in the business of making buggy whips, or you're overly content with your station in life, standing still is your last concern. As an employee in a technical company, a technical company where state-of-the-art practices are vital to overall success, it's important that you keep moving to keep abreast of new and changing developments.
   What that means is that all employees—and our engineers and scientists in particular—should continuously strive to develop and improve their skills through a commitment to "lifelong learning."
   Lifelong learning means always being intellectually curious and working to satisfy that curiosity. It doesn't mean enrolling in a college degree program. Satisfying your intellectual curiosity can mean taking a company-sponsored course, enrolling in a workshop, or attending a seminar. It can mean researching and writing a technical paper. It can also mean simply turning to someone knowledgeable in your office for an explanation of something you don't understand.
   Keep in mind that a college degree doesn't guarantee infinite wisdom. All it does is give you a set of tools and insights to begin dealing with the physical world. Once you've graduated the world doesn't stand still. Technology and techniques change and advance and—if you're interested in furthering your career— you need to keep up by enrolling in courses so that you increase your knowledge base and bring more insight to your work. You

should also consider taking courses in allied fields so that you can broaden your perspective.

Lifelong learning works for your benefit as well because as you increase your knowledge about what you're doing, you become more interested in your work, do a better job, and are viewed as a more valued employee. In turn, you set the stage for being given more challenging assignments and, of course, receive the commensurate rewards in the form of salary and advancement.

Furthermore, I would suggest lifelong learning is just plain fun because it helps you grow as an individual.

I've often stated that, as a company, we're only as good as our technology. That statement is just as applicable to every employee because, ultimately, we're only as good as all of you and how well each of you works to improve your skills and satisfy your intellectual curiosity.

You want to avoid, as does this example, a patronizing, preachy, or self-serving tone. If you have an executive who insists on writing in an obnoxious tone, you may be in a no-win position. All you can do is try to muffle the tone with judicious editing.

GUEST COLUMNISTS

A column featuring guest writers can also be a popular feature. In every issue, a different member of the organization or a different employee sounds off on something important to them. A guest column can bring important topics to the attention of employees and acquaint them with departments and company functions other than their own. The following column is from *Focus on Technology,* published for consumers and rehabilitation, employment, and eye-care professionals.

"FROM THE DOCTOR'S CORNER..."

Ophthalmologist Donald Fletcher discusses an information gap

"The greatest tragedy in vision loss today is the gap that exists between visually impaired patients and the resources available to them. A recent patient of mine illustrates this well.

A 27 year old man was referred to me for vision rehabilitation services. He had a hereditary macular condition that had resulted in a decrease in central acuity in both eyes. His vision had not caused him any functional difficulties until his senior year in high school when he noticed his reading becoming much more labored and slow. He had always been an honors student and his grades dropped slightly in his senior year. He was offered six different college scholarships but felt unable to accept any of them because of the increasing difficulty he was having reading small print. His ophthalmologist told him that nothing could be done for the condition; thus, he resigned himself to an occupation that required limited visual skills. For eight years, he worked on a loading dock at a warehouse. He would take his paperwork home at night and spend hours laboring over it.

This man literally smiled from ear-to-ear when, at age 27, he learned of the many simple and inexpensive low vision devices that could make his remaining vision more useful to him. His life aspirations took on a new direction as he realized that he would be able to accomplish the reading necessary for a college education with the help of a video magnifier CCTV.

The tragedy in this case is not that a macular condition could not be cured, but rather that eight years of a life were wasted because of not being informed of the availability of devices to help. My opthalmologic colleagues must become more aware not only of the life implications of vision loss, but also what responsibility they have to make their patients aware of the many resources available to this large group of patients. Then instead of saying, 'nothing more can be done,' doctors can start patients on the path to best utilizing their valuable asset: residual vision."

Donald C. Fletcher, M.D.
Vitreoretinal Associates
Seattle, Washington

GOSSIP COLUMNS

A social or gossip column can be a great success with readers. Such columns report personal news, such as birth and marriage announcements, news of minor achievements and awards, mentions of trips or vacations, and miscellaneous trivia that may be of interest. Gossip columns acquaint employees with one another and promote a team or family feeling in the organization. If you or one of your writers has the gift, you can make the column a humorous one. The humor must be gentle and good-natured, of course. Here, from *Crossroads*, is an example of a gossip column with a little extra twist of humor.

POTPOURRI

Terry Dunn, Scott Edwards, Bruce McGown and Janet Kao recently attended a BCA audit training class in Chicago. No one is too specific about what they learned there, however, because the flight back was a Shakey's Special with free pizza and 10 cent beer.

Reimbursement and Facility Audit was never like this.

* * *

When-will-they-ever-learn department: Lois Dahl, Group Billing, became Mrs. John Chanik, September 29th. Taking the giant step in November are Lee Webb, Data Processing, and Julie Roellich. Gary Johnson, Data Processing, and Judy Martin, formerly of Federal Programs, have set a February date.

* * *

And how's your backhand? A certain Senior Personnel Manager was noticeably silent about the King-Riggs tennis match. Seems he promoted a tennis match to raise money for his church. The female was a 13-year-old girl and carrying the standard for the "boys" was, you guessed it, our hero. The outcome bore a strong resemblance to the outcome of the King-Riggs match . . . four sets to nothing. And he even sent her flowers before the game.

* * *

Third verse of the same tune . . . the Fratts, Nubs and Carol, Enrollment, vacationed in Baja California, in September. Nubs caught a 118 lb. striped marlin for his mantel and the little woman a 121 lb. striped marlin for hers.

* * *

And for another dream of a vacation, try this on for size: Pat Livingstone, Federal Programs, spent two weeks in Mexico scuba diving.

* * *

Congratulations to Marilyn Roberts, formerly of Group Billing, who is now teaching at Lake Washington Elementary School.

* * *

Is there any significance to the fact that the Johnsons outnumber the Smiths in this Plan?

QUESTION-AND-ANSWER COLUMNS

Another popular type of column is one where readers write in seeking answers to questions. This type of column presents important information in an entertaining format. Here, from *Focus on Technology*, is an excerpt from a very practical question-and-answer column.

"ASK STEVE ..."

Q When I turn on my VersaBraille II + (VB II +), it makes a series of tones, the display pops up momentarily, then nothing else happens. What's wrong?

A The VB II + acts like this whenever it encounters a low battery condition. This can be caused by:

a. the charger was disconnected while the VB II + was on,
b. power from the wall outlet was discontinued for some period of time,
c. the charger has failed, or
d. the battery is really low.

To get the VB II + started again, press Dot 5 as you turn it on. If the charger is not plugged in and the battery really is low, then the conditions will repeat. Plug in the charger and recharge the batteries for at least 14 hours. If the charger has failed, the VB II + low-power symptoms will persist. Call TSI Customer Service.

WRITING HEADLINES

After you've written your story, you must write a headline for it. Sometimes, you may need to write a deck and subheads as well. A *deck*, also called a *kicker*, is a supplemental headline set in smaller type and positioned directly above or below the primary headline. Here are some general guidelines for writing headlines:

O Use active verbs. Write *Freeman Wins Sales Award* not *Sales Award Won by Freeman*.

O Use the present tense. Write *B. F. Smythington Retires* not *B. F. Smythington Retired*. If the event is in the future, write *B. F. Smythington to Retire*.

O Use short words. Write *Work Starts on New Office* not *Construction Begins on Headquarters Building*.

O Be specific. Write *Greene to Head Advertising* not *New Department Director Named*.

O Be straightforward. Avoid puns, word play, and rhymes.

Here are some examples of good headlines:

Maung Soe Myint Receives Award for Volunteerism

Drive to Benefit Women's Crisis Center

Funding Available for 1990 Arts Projects

Heath Introduces Innovative Reading Program

Picnic '88!

Presto Westo Means Magic

Help us Kill-a-Watt

If your story is lengthy, include subheads in the body to break it up into manageable segments so that it's not so intimidating to the readers. If you want the headline to contain more information than normal, include a deck, as in the following example:

Last of a Flying Breed:
Final DSCS II Is Readied for Launch

*   *   *

Home Equity Loans
Good Interest Rates and Tax Breaks

Effective headlines lure readers into your stories and make them want to read more.

SUMMARY

Personality profiles and columns can add a lot of human interest to your newsletter. The important points covered in this chapter include:

1. Use your discretion when deciding how much personal information to include in a personality profile.

2. Find a focus for your personality profile, such as a single unifying theme that runs through the subject's life or, on the other hand, a surprising contrast.

3. For a personality profile, use a lead that alerts the readers to the focus or theme of the story.

4. Use a column written by management to bring important topics to the attention of employees but be careful to avoid a lecturing or patronizing tone.

5. Use a column featuring guest writers to introduce important topics and acquaint employees with other departments and functions in the organization.

6. Use a gossip column to acquaint employees with each other and promote a team or family feeling.

7. Use a question-and-answer column to present important information in an entertaining format.

8. When writing headlines, use active verbs, the present tense, and short, specific, straightforward words.

Chapter 6 gives guidelines for crafting stories with language that's both strong and clear.

Writing with Clarity and Strength

KEEPING PARAGRAPHS SHORT

USING ACTIVE VERBS

CHOOSING PLAIN LANGUAGE

USING CLEAR TRANSITIONS

BEING SPECIFIC AND CONCRETE

NAMING YOUR SOURCES

USING CREATIVE WRITING DEVICES

Although there are obvious differences, writing for a newsletter is similar to writing for other periodicals. The techniques that make prose vigorous and colorful in a newspaper or magazine article also make prose vigorous and colorful in a newsletter story. Keep paragraphs short, use active verbs, choose plain language, use clear transitions, be specific and concrete, name your sources, and use creative writing devices.

KEEPING PARAGRAPHS SHORT

Studies show that readers absorb short chunks of information better than long ones. And, if you run long on content and short on space, short paragraphs give you more flexibility as you cut and shape the story to fit.

Here's an example of an announcement that needs to be broken up into shorter paragraphs.

REGISTER TO VOTE

Starting next week, Warden employees who have recently
moved to the area, changed addresses, or have never registered
to vote will be able to sign up with Bartlett County and Fisher
County registrars. Registrars for Bartlett County will be in the
employee lounge at the Central office on Wednesday, April 20,
and Wednesday, April 27, from 11:30 a.m. until 2:30 p.m.
Registrars for both Bartlett and Fisher Counties will be in the
lunchroom at the Country Acres Office on Wednesday, May 4,
and Wednesday, May 11, from 11:30 a.m. until 2:00 p.m. If you
plan to register, be sure to have some proof of identity, such as a
driver's license, with you.

In the following rewrite, you can see how much easier
the announcement is to read when the paragraphs are
shortened.

REGISTER TO VOTE

Starting next week, Warden employees who have recently
moved to the area, changed addresses, or have never registered
to vote will be able to sign up with Bartlett County and Fisher
County registrars.

Registrars for Bartlett County will be in the employee lounge
at the Central office on Wednesday, April 20, and Wednesday,
April 27, from 11:30 a.m. until 2:30 p.m.

Registrars for both Bartlett and Fisher Counties will be in the
lunchroom at the Country Acres Office on Wednesday, May 4,
and Wednesday, May 11, from 11:30 a.m. until 2:00 p.m.

If you plan to register, be sure to have some proof of identity,
such as a driver's license, with you.

USING ACTIVE VERBS

You can make your stories lively and gripping with one
simple technique: use active verbs. With *active verbs*, the
subject takes the action. With *passive verbs*, the subject is
acted on. Here are some examples:

Active verb:

Water *flooded* the basement.

Passive verb:

The basement *was flooded* with water.

Active verb:

Governor Jones *signed* the bill in a ceremony yesterday.

Passive verb:

The bill *was signed* by Governor Jones in a ceremony yesterday.

Active verb:

Underground explosions *weakened* the foundations.

Passive verb:

The foundations *have been weakened* by underground explosions.

Keep an eye out for such deadening state-of-being verbs as:

is	is being
was	are being
are	have been
were	be

Replace these verbs with active verbs that will make your stories forceful and direct, as in the following examples:

Active verb:

Tiger boosters *led* a rally in the lobby Tuesday.

Passive verb:

The lobby *was* the site of a rally led by Tiger boosters Tuesday.

Active verb:

C. B. Jenkins *leads* the move for centralization.

Passive verb:

The move for centralization *is being led* by C. B. Jenkins.

CHOOSING PLAIN LANGUAGE

Short words get your message across economically, plain words are easier to understand, and where newsletter writing is concerned, less is more. Here are some guidelines:

○ Use plain words and avoid fancy multisyllable ones like *ascertain, prioritize, methodology, expedite.* Their shorter counterparts—*find out, rank, method,* and *speed up*—save space and sound better.

○ Watch out for noun clusters. Use the word *classroom* instead of *structured learning environment.*

○ Avoid prepositional phrases. Use *for* and *because* instead of *in the amount of* and *as a result of.*

○ Don't be redundant. Use *small* instead of *small in size.* Use *end* instead of *final conclusion.*

Here's a list of fancy words and phrases to watch out for along with the simple ones that you should use instead.

USE	INSTEAD OF
best, most	optimum
end	expiration
find out	ascertain
give	disseminate
is, makes up	constitutes
many	appreciable
most	the majority of
now	at this point in time
obvious	readily apparent
speed up	expedite

Need to cut out those noun clusters? First you have to recognize them. Here are some examples.

USE	INSTEAD OF
good, excellent	state of the art
mistake	quality reduction factor
problems	design constraints considerations

Prepositional phrases give everyone problems.

USE	INSTEAD OF
about	of the order of magnitude
because	as a result of
for	for the purpose of
for	in the amount of
know	aware of the fact that
more	in excess of
must	it is essential that
to	in order to

Redundancies can clutter your writing. Here are some examples.

USE	INSTEAD OF
available	currently available
consensus	general consensus
essential, necessary	absolutely essential
introduce	first introduce
oval	oval in shape
reason	reason why
result	end result
spell out, explain	spell out in detail

The following extract is an example of a wordy paragraph.

YOUTH COMMISSION AIDS YOUNG WRITERS

As a part of their plan to foster self-motivation and creative thought processes in preadolescent and adolescent young people, the Smithton Youth Commission will make monies available to local youth groups for creative writing projects. The intent of the plan is to encourage local fiction creating students while providing quality literary experiences for Smithton residents. Community focused projects are especially desirable.

Here's the same paragraph written in plain language.

YOUTH COMMISSION AIDS YOUNG WRITERS

The Smithton Youth Commission announced today that it has funds available for local youth groups for creative writing projects. The grants will not only encourage young writers but give people in the community a chance to read the works of fresh young writers. Projects featuring Smithton will be especially appreciated.

USING CLEAR TRANSITIONS

Transitions aren't important when you're using the telegraphic writing style (discussed in Chapter 3, "Choosing a Suitable Writing Style"), but they're vital when you're using either the personal or the semiformal writing styles. The four basic kinds of transitions are

1. support

2. contrast

3. muzzle

4. conclusion

SUPPORT-TYPE TRANSITIONS

Support-type transitions sustain or enhance the train of thought you've established for your readers. Here are examples of support-type transition words and phrases:

what is more	in addition
moreover	not only
furthermore	further
considering	since
also	besides
now	

In this excerpt from a story in *Focus on Technology*, the word *also* in the second paragraph moves the readers along while letting them know that equipment is still the topic.

"Being a fluent braille reader, I find it much easier to work in braille rather than speech-output devices. I used Dectalk before, but I found it very difficult to use to write a program. My wife and I are considering setting up our own word processing and desktop publishing company. If we do that, I would find BIT extremely helpful."

Bruce also uses an Optacon to read the telephone directory, dictionary, newspaper, and journal articles.

CONTRAST-TYPE TRANSITIONS

Contrast-type transitions turn the readers' train of thought in a different direction. Here are examples of contrast-type transition words and phrases:

but	however
in contrast	yet
conversely	on the other hand
meanwhile	

In this excerpt from a story in *60 + Newsletter*, profiling television personality Betty White, the word *however* in the second paragraph turns the readers' attention to a new facet of the same subject.

They ran out of options and called her anyway. And of course, she was a natural. (Interviewers who asked her late husband how close Betty was to the "neighborhood nymphomaniac" got the answer: "They're exactly the same, except Sue Ann cooks and Betty can't.") Moreover, audience response was so overwhelming, she was written into the series and for the next two seasons won back-to-back Emmys for her portrayal of the catty Nivens.

As Rose, however, Betty's pulled in her claws, and faces the world. . . .

MUZZLE-TYPE TRANSITIONS

Muzzle-type transitions qualify information or opinions for the readers. Sometimes, they say to readers, "Wait a minute before coming to a conclusion, there's another perspective you need to hear about." Here are examples of muzzle-type transition words and phrases:

despite	certainly
although	while
regardless	contrary to
except	

In this excerpt from *Chip & Holly's Newsletter*, the word *though* in the second paragraph brakes the train of thought. To understand the subtle effect of the transition, try reading the paragraph without it.

> On the other hand, he's a natural as the Nutcracker prince.
> And if he isn't too tall, he'll try for a third comeback this year.
> As for the future, though, Dominick's not quite so sure he
> wants to spend it all dancing. He says he likes art, and thinks....

CONCLUSION-TYPE TRANSITIONS

Conclusion-type transitions take two or more lines of thought and pull them into focus for the readers. Here are some examples of conclusion-type transitions:

thus	therefore
consequently	in conclusion
finally	so

In this excerpt from *WRQuarterly*, the transition word *so* in the second paragraph wraps up the article.

And on Thursday night, August 11, WRQ will be hosting a party at Wet n' Wild Water Park. There will be a buffet dinner, beer, wine and pop, dancing and plenty of fun for the little kid in all of us. Complimentary bus service will be available from both hotels for the 7:00 pm to midnight event.

So come by our booths. See our new products, get your questions answered and pick up your Wet n' Wild tickets. We'll see you in Orlando.

BEING SPECIFIC AND CONCRETE

When choosing words, be as specific as possible. Give the readers concrete facts, not vague impressions. You've heard of the ladder of abstraction? Well, you want to get right down to the bottom of it. You'll write not about the dog who is the scientist's constant companion, but about the liver-and-white Pointer named Spot who accompanies the scientist to the grocery store, the barber shop, and the lab.

If you write about a heat wave, tell readers that temperatures were over 110° Fahrenheit for ten days in August and that the pavement cracked and the asphalt bubbled. Don't give them the bland news that the days were hot or the temperatures were high for several days.

In the following excerpt from *Kent Arts*, the writer could have generalized and said something like: "China is home to a large number of minority groups." The story, however, includes specific detail that gives the reader a much better idea of the variety offered in the exhibit.

China is home to 55 national minority groups. Of the nearly one billion people in China, 56 million belong to one of these minorities. Many of the 42 prints in this exhibit illustrate the cultural activities and colorful costumes of these varied peoples.

NAMING YOUR SOURCES

As mentioned in Chapter 2, "Gathering News," the facts in your stories must be accurate. In most organizations, the readers can assume that the newsletter staff has access to inside information. But there are times when you should reassure readers that you do indeed know what you're talking about. Note your sources when you're announcing something of great significance or, as in the following excerpt from *Focus on Technology*, when you want to give evidence to support a point. The writer could have said something like this: "The four reservationists are getting rave reviews." Instead, the writer backs up the statement by giving the source of the information.

> At TWA in New York City, four determined blind and low vision people have become full-time reservationists. They are accessing PCs which emulate TWA's PLARS terminals with Vista, Vert, and/or VersaBraille II + (for large print, speech, and braille). In the April 16 "Travel Weekly" cover article, Training Supervisor John McQueeney says that in competitive performance reviews, Carlos Gomez, Gloria Morelli, Elba Santiago, and Mark Simitian "all drew outstanding marks for bookings made and revenues produced."

If you can't verify information, you need to print it with a qualification so that readers realize that the information may or may not be factual. Some common qualifiers are

It is believed that. . . .

According to several sources. . . .

It is Smith's opinion that. . . .

It was Smith's understanding that. . . .

Be very careful that your qualifiers get the job done, however. In the following example, the first version gives readers the impression that the restructuring of the marketing department will definitely take place. The second version is more accurate because it qualifies the statement.

Version 1:

Smyth-Brown said the marketing department would be restructured next year.

Version 2:

Smyth-Brown said he understood that the marketing department would be restructured next year.

USING CREATIVE WRITING DEVICES

I have vague memories of English 101. Our instructor touched on a number of rhetorical devices, things like similes and literary allusion, that seemed useless to me at the time. Well, over the years, similes, allusions, and other devices for jazzing up writing have become infinitely more important. Used sparingly, they can move your writing from the mundane to the memorable, like a fine sauce turning a bland dish into something more tasty. This section describes and gives examples of the following creative writing devices: questions; allusions; epigrams; anecdotes; metaphors, similes, and analogies; and direct address.

QUESTIONS

When was the last time you read an article because it began with a question that piquéd your curiosity? A question makes a personal connection from the writer directly to the reader. You can use this device either in the lead or in the body to draw your reader into the story. In the following example from *Crossroads*, the question ends the story.

> The seven danger signals of cancer. They have been well publicized in magazines . . . and on radio . . . and TV. We all know what they are.
> Or do we?

Here, from *BPM Newswave*, is another example.

> I'd like to introduce you to Gabrielle Greeley, assistant manager of Westwood Village Apts, Irving. Gabrielle has distinguished herself by closing out three of the four past months with ZERO delinquencies. How does she do it? She has lots of determination, commitment, and a tremendous desire to succeed at whatever she attempts.

ALLUSIONS

Literary allusions are probably more common than any of us realize. Some allusions have become so much a part of popular culture that we take them for granted. Very few of us remember that "They also serve who only stand and wait" comes from Milton, but the allusion has great resonance for those who do remember it as one of Winston Churchill's stirring wartime messages. Most of us find allusions to the Gettysburg Address meaningful, but for those who hear the Miltonic and biblical rhythms in the address itself, the allusions are even richer. We hear many allusions to President Kennedy's addresses, and his words are full of allusions themselves—to Abraham Lincoln's words among others.

But, you may ask, how can you use literary allusions in a newsletter for business people or machinists or hobbyists? Well, you can not only use literary allusions, you can also use allusions to other aspects of our shared culture, such as the lyrics from songs, fictional or historical characters, films, stage plays, and so on. Read the following sampling from a dozen newsletters around the country.

Allusions in Headlines:

A Connecticut Yankee's Christmas Missive

The Boy Who Would Be Prince

Fab Photos

A Day in the Life of . . .

A Man for All Seasons

"It's a Family Affair"

"How the West Was Won"!

Odd Couple—Texas Style

"For Kids From One to Ninety-Two . . ."

Food for Thought: A Lecture Series with International Flavor

Allusions in Stories:

Third verse of the same tune . . . the Fratts, Nubs and Carol, Enrollment, vacationed in Baja, California, in September.

* * *

Babe Ruths they're not, but as these accompanying photographs show, the fellows on our Blue Cross softball team play a hard, fast, and enthusiastic game of slow-pitch.

* * *

Some people make things look easy. Larry Bird and basketball. Bob Vila and old houses. Robin Williams and improvisation.

EPIGRAMS

An *epigram* is a meaningful quotation that states the theme or sets the mood right at the beginning of a story. This example from *The Sentinel* uses not one but three epigrams.

S&D Retirements:
Changing of the Guard

"The torch has been passed to a new generation of
Americans ..."

—John F. Kennedy

"Time and tide wait for no man."

—Geoffrey Chaucer

"Retirement at 65 is ridiculous. When I was 65, I still had
pimples."

—George Burns

ANECDOTES

As mentioned in Chapter 5, "Writing Personality Profiles
and Columns," an anecdote makes a fine lead for a story,
especially a personality profile. You can also use an anecdote to make a point in the body of a story.

The following example shows how the *BPM Newswave*
used an anecdote in a story about the effectiveness of a
promotional device.

BEST OF THE BEST

Donna Cocke
Manager, Knollwood Village

"The Best of The Best"—that's what we say in the Midwest
District. The buttons we wear spread the message everywhere
we go. To prove our point, leasing consultant Debbie Clolinger,
Knollwood Village Apts (Grand Blanc, MI), had her "BOTB" pin
on when she took our daily deposit to the bank. She made quite a
commotion. People were asking her what it meant. She calmly
answered, "I work for Knollwood and WE ARE the Best of the
Best." When Debbie reached teller Amy Daniels, Amy asked her
what was so "best" about Knollwood Village. Debbie said, "Let
me show you." Amy made an appointment for later that day.
Needless to say, after the "grand tour," Amy is a new resident.

This excerpt from a story in *CSC Update* is another example of how to use an anecdote.

THE VOLUNTEER CHORE MINISTRY

When a 68 year old woman broke her leg and needed light housekeeping and laundry assistance, her volunteer was a 77 year old woman who was driven to her house by yet another volunteer . . . five volunteers taking turns driving an elderly woman to see her husband every day at a nursing home, and then taking her back that evening.

SIMILES, METAPHORS, AND ANALOGIES

A simile is a brief comparison of one thing to another. *A voice like a tiger's purr. He looked like he had swallowed a canary.* Some similes, like the last one, are so familiar that they have become cliches and should be avoided. Fresh similes, however, make your writing meaningful and energetic. Here, from *60 + Newsletter*, is an example of a simile.

The hair's full and cropped short, and her skin—like a porcelain doll's—is a pale translucent.

A *metaphor*, instead of comparing one thing to another, turns one thing into something else so that we see it differently or see certain elements of it more vividly. Some metaphors are simple: *The wind stirs the trees. He flashes a smile. The audience roared its approval.* Other metaphors are more complex: *The committee is swimming in a sea of confusion. There's a blight on this project.* Here are four examples of metaphors, the first two from *Chip & Holly's Newsletter* and the last two from *The Sentinel*.

With this strategy, the young dancer chased away the butterflies and settled himself into the star role of the Nutcracker Prince for two seasons straight.

*   *   *

We just found out about the Kentucky Fried Chicken/Good Housekeeping greeting card contest, and if you hurry, you can get in under the wire.

*   *   *

Innovation is the fuel of TRW's future; the driver in a never-ending quest to be the best.

*   *   *

Last year Robinson's story was splashed across the pages of Los Angeles-area newspapers when he crash-landed his disabled aircraft in a suburban neighborhood.

An extended metaphor becomes an *analogy*. An analogy can bring otherwise dead descriptions to living, breathing life. An analogy also helps an explanation because it shows how something readers are not familiar with is similar to something they are familiar with. Here are two examples of analogies, from the *60 + Newsletter* and *Northwest DANCE Focus*, respectively.

The resultant *American Country Inn and Bed & Breakfast Cookbook* is one part cookbook, one part travel guide, with a pinch of occasional folklore thrown in for good measure.

*   *   *

It was in the last few days in Singapore, a potpourri of Asian cultures with a distinctive Singaporean flavor of its own, that I realized we are watching a fetus grow, sometimes coordinated and, at other times, not, working its way through the various influences and internal needs. The trip raised more questions in my mind than it answered, and I am looking forward to returning to watch the child grow up into its own and find its idiom.

DIRECT ADDRESS

When you address your readers directly, you draw them into the story and make them a part of it. This excerpt from *BPM Newswave* is an example of direct address.

> It is important for you to know the procedure to follow in case of an emergency. Know how and to whom to report a fire or any other emergency. Know where fire alarms, fire extinguishers, emergency equipment and telephones are located. Check floor plans and exits and plan an evacuation route. Your local fire department will be glad to give you assistance.

Just to show you how direct address gives a story immediacy and makes it more personal, I have taken the liberty of rewriting the story in the third person.

> It is important to know the procedure to follow in case of an emergency. Everyone should know how and to whom to report a fire or any other emergency. Everyone should also know where fire alarms, fire extinguishers, emergency equipment and telephones are located. It is also important to check floor plans and exits and plan an evacuation route. The local fire department can give assistance in making these plans if anyone should need it.

SUMMARY

Choosing language that is strong and clear gives your stories energy and punch. The important points in this chapter are

1. Keep paragraphs short.
2. Use active rather than passive verbs.

3. Choose plain language by avoiding multisyllable words, noun clusters, prepositional phrases, and redundancies.

4. Use clear transitions that can be support-type, enhancing the current topic; contrast-type, turning to a new topic; muzzle-type, qualifying the topic; or conclusion-type, pulling two or more lines of thought into focus.

5. Choose specific, concrete words rather than general, abstract words.

6. Name the sources of your information.

7. Use creative writing devices such as questions, allusions, epigrams, anecdotes, metaphors, similes, analogies, and direct address.

For more information on writing, see the list of reference books in "Resources" at the end of this book.

Chapter 7 describes how to create a style guide to ensure consistency and also discusses proofreading.

Creating a Style Guide and Proofreading

CREATING A STYLE GUIDE

PROOFREADING

You, of course, want to protect your newsletter from any errors and inconsistencies that could dim its luster. Using a style guide and proofreading make up your best defense. A style guide adds polish and makes editing easier and faster. And, with a little know-how and practice, careful proofreading becomes second nature. Using a style guide and proofreading will also save you the unnecessary aggravation of telephone calls and notes pointing out the mistakes in the latest issue of your newsletter.

CREATING A STYLE GUIDE

Save yourself a lot of time and trouble and create a style guide for your newsletter. A *style guide* contains rules for spelling, punctuation, using numbers, and grammar. In addition to the guide, which contains rules specific to your newsletter, you should own a style manual, a good dictionary, and a book on grammar, where you can find answers to the questions that will inevitably arise. ("Resources," at the end of this book, lists some excellent reference books.) For instance, is *database* one word or two?

Should you write *BA* or *B.A.?* What is the possessive of *CRT?* Then, every time you are uncertain about a usage and look it up, you can add the correct form to the style guide, where it will be easy to find next time.

Your style guide should include guidelines for spelling, punctuation, capitalization, hyphenation, and, if they're relevant to your newsletter, rules for using numbers.

SPELLING

Inevitably, certain words are sure to crop up again and again in your newsletter and you might as well find out, once and for all, the correct spelling, including capitalization, hyphenation, and how to make plurals. Look the word up or check on it, and record the correct spelling in your style guide.

NAMES.   You need to include the correct spelling for any names that will appear regularly in your newsletter. People can be quite sensitive about having their names misspelled. I came close to committing this unpardonable error once. A vice-president in our organization had a middle initial, not a middle *name*, but a middle initial that stood alone without a period behind it. Let's call him Franklin A Jones. In the past he had complained loudly about his name being misspelled, but I was new and unaware. Luckily, one of my co-workers caught my error and removed the offensive period. A style guide would have been a big help, and after this incident, we put one together.

You should also include the correct form for titles and the correct names of departments, other companies, and any products peculiar to your field or business.

TERMS.   Certain terms are probably common in your organization. If you're in the computer business, you may have to know whether *filename* is one word or two. If you're in the motivation business, you should know whether you write *Positive Mental Attitude* with initial capital letters or not. Or, perhaps you're in the communications business and need to know the plural for the word *antenna*. Add the correct spelling for common terms to your style guide.

PROBLEM WORDS.   Some words are problem words for everyone. *Accommodate, collectible,* and *referred* are examples of words that often appear in lists of commonly misspelled words. Other words may be your own particular problem children. If you find yourself going to the dictionary to look up a word more than once, add it to your style guide.

NUMBERS AND SYMBOLS

You may use a lot of numbers in your field. You may need to know how to write percentages or hyphenate fractions, or how to use symbols for degrees and angles. Or you may need to know how to write scientific notation. Include whatever guidelines you feel will be necessary.

PUNCTUATION

Although you'll be able to look up the rules of punctuation in your reference book, you have some decisions to make. For instance, how will you punctuate items in a series? How will you punctuate captions for photographs and illustrations? Answer these questions in your style guide.

ITEMS IN A SERIES.   Today, most people put a comma before the words *and* or *or*, after the next-to-last item in a series. Here's an example:

> You can also add a friendly menu manager, a calculator, and a voice prompter.

Whether you decide to use the comma before the word *and* or not, the important thing is to choose one way or the other and then do it consistently.

HEADLINES.   Include the style you'll use for headlines in your guide. You can capitalize the first letter of every word, except for articles and prepositions that have five or fewer letters, or you can capitalize only the first letter of the first word. The trend today is toward the latter style.

Murphy to head Dayton branch

CAPTIONS.   How will you handle captions under photographs and illustrations? You should decide on some standard guidelines and then follow them consistently. The following guidelines are typical.

O Use initial caps in the title (which is optional) and end it with a period.

O Punctuate and capitalize the legend (descriptive material) like any normal sentence in the text. This rule applies whether the legend is made up of complete sentences or sentence fragments.

O Enclose the photo credit in parentheses and end it without a period.

This is a typical caption.

Dancer in Action. Sylvie Phillips performs at the Community Mime Theatre
July 15–22. (Photo: Nora Johnson)

You can see how other editors handle captions in the reproductions of newsletters appearing later in this book.

A SAMPLE STYLE GUIDE

The following is an example of a style guide for a newsletter
published by a software company for its employees.

SPELLING AND ABBREVIATIONS

AT	NEC Multispeed ELX
BASIC	NEC Multispeed HD
CBT	NEC Multispeed LCD
compatible	O/S
CPU	OEM
Diconix 150P	OEMs
disk controller	OMEGA
diskettes	OS/2
filename	PC Works
IBM	RAM
MACH 20	retrieval
megabytes	Spell command
Micro D	Windows
MS DOS	

NAMES

C. B. Cannon   Regina R. King
Phyllis Carter   D. B. St. John
Paula Des Prez   Carter Brown-Smythe
Arthur Martin Green

GUIDELINES

Hyphenate adjectives in front of the word they modify.
> out-of-pocket cost
> double-disk drive

Spell out an acronym on first mention.
> Original Equipment Manufacturer (OEM)

Use lower case for time designations.
> 7:00 am; 7:30 pm

CAPITALIZATION

Capitalize titles that appear before the name.
> Vice President Brown

Do not capitalize position titles that appear after the name.
> Janice Brown, vice president

Capitalize names of departments.
> Marketing

NUMBERS AND SYMBOLS

640K

Spell out *percent, and, at,* and *number* rather than using %, &, @, and #.
> ninety percent, trial and error,
> five at $6.00 each, the number of runs,

Spell out numbers ten and under.
> The fight went three rounds.

Use figures for numbers over ten.
> They completed 11 versions.

Use figures when a sentence includes numbers both under and over ten.
> She needed 3 copies of each of the 15 documents.

Use a figure when it makes more sense.
> The series included 20 million items.

PUNCTUATION

Put a comma before *and* or *or* in a series of three or more.
> You can choose one option, all options, or no options.

NAMES AND MODES OF ADDRESS

Give the full name on first mention.
> Alice G. Wright is named president.

Use the last name thereafter in news stories.
> Wright comes from Chanute.

Use the first name thereafter in features like
personality profiles.

> Alice comes from Chanute.

Follow an employee's name with the name of his or
her department.

> Alice G. Wright, Marketing

Don't use Mr., Ms, or Mrs.

HEADLINES AND CAPTIONS

Use initial caps for headlines except for articles and
prepositions that have five or fewer letters.

> ABC Begins the President's Race

Punctuate all captions even when they're incomplete
sentences.

> George Warren and Ann Montgomery at
> Comp-Tel.

REFERENCES

The Chicago Manual of Style

Webster's Dictionary

PROOFREADING

Who does what on your newsletter depends on the size and
makeup of your staff. Traditionally, a copy editor and a
proofreader check for different things. But typically, on a
newsletter, everyone on the staff proofreads everyone else's
copy. This much is sure: someone other than the writer of
a story should proofread it. If you are a one-person operation, try to prevail on a co-worker or a friend to proofread
your copy for you.

When you proofread:

O Check for spelling, grammar, and punctuation.

O Check for adherence to the style guide.

O Look for typos, of course, and mistakes.

O Check names in the captions and headlines against the names in the text.

O Check to see that the specifications have been followed, that body copy, headlines, and captions are set in correct type style and size. (Chapter 11, "Designing Your Newsletter," discusses specifications.)

Whoever proofreads, edits, or revises manuscripts should be familiar with standard proofreader's marks. Figure 7-1 outlines them in full. Figure 7-2 shows a page of marked-up text as an example of how to use the marks. Using a colored pencil, write the changes beside the flawed line, in the margin closest to the error. When you have two or more corrections in a line, list them from left to right and separate them by slant lines. Print substitutions in the margin and then put a caret (^) in the line to mark the place where the substitution should go. If you have to delete a character, a word, or words, put a delete mark in the margin and a line through the text that should be deleted.

PROOFREADERS' MARKS	IN MARGIN	IN TEXT
Insert period	⊙	M̬D.
comma	⸜	St. Louis͏ͅMO
colon	♦	For͏ͅ
semicolon	⁏	late͏ͅtherefore
apostrophe	⌄	hasn͏ͅt appeared
quotation marks	⌄ / ⌄⌄	͏ͅYes,͏ͅhe replied
hyphen	/=/	white͏ͅwater basin
parentheses	(/)	listed.͏ͅSee Figures.͏ͅ
dash	⌐m	arrested͏ͅthe time before
ellipsis	# ⊙ # ⊙ # ⊙	singing͏ͅWalker
space	#	lesson͏ͅ18
Paragraph	¶	lessons.¶Clients will
No paragraph	No ¶	⌐ The next
Run in on same line	(Run in)	Before you⌐start basting the roast
Insert here	for / and	Watch out͏ͅmoisture͏ͅdust
Make superscript	⌄2	(x ⌄2)
Make subscript	⌃2	(x ⌃2)
Transpose	(tr) / (tr)	a brihgt morning spring
Close up	⌢	Ph.͏ͅD.
Spell out	(sp)	finish④or more
Delete	e / e	twoø of the candidates
Use lower case	(l.c.)	the last Ɖelivery
		the AƉRIATIC
Use capital letter	(cap)	͏ͅcenterville, Nebraska
Use small capitals	(s.c.)	9:00 a̲.m̲.
Set in roman	(Rom)	the filly (Carmen)
Set in italics	(ital)	the word elevator
Set in boldface	(b.f.)	Note: Extreme Heat
Let it stand (ignore marks)	(stet)	time and time again

Figure 7-1. Proofreaders' marks

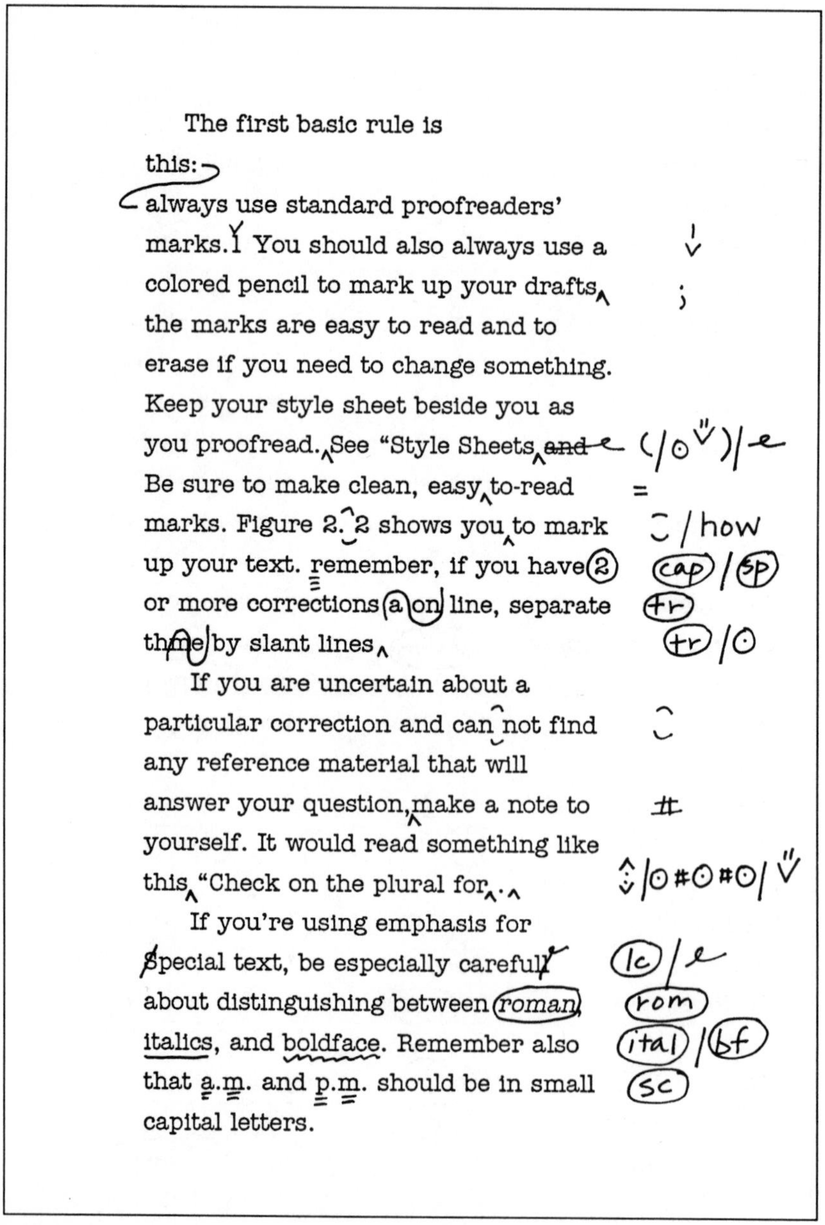

The first basic rule is this: always use standard proofreaders' marks. You should also always use a colored pencil to mark up your drafts, the marks are easy to read and to erase if you need to change something. Keep your style sheet beside you as you proofread. See "Style Sheets, and Be sure to make clean, easy to-read marks. Figure 2. 2 shows you to mark up your text. remember, if you have 2 or more corrections a on line, separate them by slant lines.

If you are uncertain about a particular correction and can not find any reference material that will answer your question, make a note to yourself. It would read something like this, "Check on the plural for.

If you're using emphasis for special text, be especially careful about distinguishing between roman, italics, and boldface. Remember also that a.m. and p.m. should be in small capital letters.

Figure 7-2. An example of marked-up text

SUMMARY

Creating a style guide for your newsletter and carefully proofreading it not only make your newsletter easier to read, they also make your work easier. The important points in this chapter are

1. Your style guide should cover the spelling of any problematic words that you use regularly in your newsletter, such as names and titles of company officials, names of departments, terms common to your field, and just plain hard-to-spell words.

2. Include the proper way to write numbers and symbols if you use them in your newsletter.

3. Set the standards for punctuating items in a series and captions.

4. Always have your copy proofread by more than one person.

5. Use standard proofreaders' marks.

Chapter 8 discusses photos—where to get them, what kind of equipment and supplies you need, how to take good ones, and how to get good-quality prints.

CHAPTER 8

Using Photographs

SOURCES FOR PHOTOGRAPHS

EQUIPMENT AND SUPPLIES

TAKING PHOTOGRAPHS

GETTING FINISHED PRINTS

Photographs are to newsletters what whipped cream is to pumpkin pie; you can do without it, but why would you want to? Photos add human interest and graphic variety to your newsletter, so include them whenever you can. Even if you're reproducing your newsletter on a photocopy machine, try to include a photograph occasionally. The reproduction won't be great, but your readers will appreciate it anyway.

SOURCES FOR PHOTOGRAPHS

You can obtain photos for your newsletter in a number of ways:

- O Your reporters can serve as photographers.
- O Employees of the organization who are camera buffs can cover events for you in exchange for a credit line.
- O You may be able to get glossy black-and-white photos from the company library.

○ Public libraries and museums often are sources of photographs. (If the photographs are copyrighted, you'll need permission.)

○ Newspapers will usually give you prints of photos that relate to your organization.

○ A photography class or club in a high school, community college, or university might take assignments from you.

USING CREDIT LINES

Always use a credit line under a photo, giving the name of the photographer. Usually, the credit line appears in parentheses after the caption. If you prefer, you can list all the contributors, including the photographers, in a box in the newsletter.

LABELING PHOTOGRAPHS

To avoid losing important information, label each photo as soon as you receive it. Writing on the back of the photograph will damage it, so write or type the information on a gummed label and then stick it on the back of the photo. You need to record

1. the date the photo was taken,
2. an identification or description of the subject matter, and
3. the name of the photographer.

DIRECTING PHOTOGRAPHERS

To get successful photos that fill your needs, give photographers the following information before sending them out on a photo session.

- O Describe the story, its subject, its importance, and how the photographs will support it.
- O Name the subjects and describe the situation you want to illustrate.
- O Describe several scenes that might work.
- O State the size and paper surface you need.
- O Give the time and date of the shooting.
- O Give the time and date that you need prints and/or enlargements.
- O List any caption information the photographer is responsible for.

GETTING RELEASES

If the photograph appears only in your newsletter, you don't need to get a model release from any of the people in it. Of course, you wouldn't use photos that would embarrass anyone.

EQUIPMENT AND SUPPLIES

If you choose to take your own photographs rather than relying on volunteers or stock photos, you'll need camera equipment and supplies.

CAMERA EQUIPMENT

You can go broke buying camera equipment—lenses, filters, tripods—or you can operate satisfactorily with one compact, autofocus 35-mm camera. Decide what you need and can afford for your newsletter.

SINGLE-LENS-REFLEX 35-MM CAMERA. A single-lens-reflex (SLR) 35-mm camera lets you interchange lenses for full flexibility. This type of camera is available in a wide price range with a wide variety of options. You need skill and experience for best results. If you have creative urges, this type of camera is what you want.

You can get many types of lenses for the SLR 35-mm camera: zoom, macro, superfast, and ultrawide. The shorter the focal length, the greater the angle of view. You can choose from many focal lengths, ranging from the fish-eye 8-mm f2.8 (angle of view 180°) to 35-mm–105-mm zoom f3.5 (angle of view 62°–23°) to 105-mm f2.5 (angle of view 23°). For your purposes, a zoom lens with a range of either 35 mm–70 mm or 40 mm–80 mm should do very well. To get the sharpest photos, use a camera with a glass rather than a plastic lens.

AUTOMATIC 35-MM CAMERA WITH MANUAL OVERRIDE. An automatic 35-mm camera equipped with manual override and a flash lets you take satisfactory pictures under a variety of circumstances and at a good range of distances. Because it has autofocus and autowind, snapping pictures rapidly when the occasion demands it is easy. Then, when you have more time to compose your pictures, you can switch to manual. This type of camera would admirably suit most newsletter publishers' needs.

AUTOMATIC 35-MM CAMERA.   An automatic camera with a flash is satisfactory for most pictures, as long as your subject is 5 to 20 feet away. You'll get good results under most normal conditions.

POLAROID CAMERA.   If you're limited to a Polaroid, your prints will not be as good as with a 35-mm camera, but they will be adequate. You do have the advantage of being able to see instantly if the shot is what you need.

FILM

Whether you take black-and-white or color photographs, you should try several brands and speeds of film. Do some experimenting and then, to get predictable results, choose one brand and one speed.

Film is categorized by its speed, depending on its ASA (or ISO) rating. Fast film can cope with many different light conditions and produces a coarser-grained print than slow film. The slower the film, the more light you'll need and the finer and sharper your print will be.

BLACK-AND-WHITE FILM.   In black-and-white film, 650 ASA is a fast film often chosen by news photographers. A medium film (125 ASA) is best when the light level is bright, and slow film (50–25 ASA) is best for bright light and long exposures.

For a newsletter, 400 ASA film will give you both flexibility and quality.

COLOR FILM.   The different brands of color film have their own characteristics. Some produce excellent skin tones, others smooth tonal qualities. So, if you use color, it's important to try several brands to find one that gives you the results you want.

Generally, you need a fast film (400–1000 ASA) that will give you good results under a variety of conditions.

TAKING PHOTOGRAPHS

Taking your own photographs is fun and satisfies the creative impulse. Even if you've never used a camera in your life, you can learn to take satisfactory photos for your newsletter with practice and experimentation. Look for instruction manuals in camera shops and bookstores ("Resources," at the end of this book, lists *The New 35mm Photographer's Handbook*, a good reference book.)

COMPOSING YOUR SHOTS

Judicious cropping can do a lot to improve a photo after you've taken it. However, you do need good material to work with, so here are some guidelines to remember when you're composing your shots.

- Visualize the picture you want to use for your story.
- Fill the frame with the picture you visualize by moving in on the subject.
- Use a focal point that is off-center to make your photo seem more alive.
- Compose your photo in thirds, not halves. Watch out for horizons that cut photos in half horizontally and things like columns or light poles that cut photos in half vertically.
- Watch out for series of objects or people in straight lines. Curved lines are easier for the eye to follow.

O Use people in shots, even when the subject is inanimate (a building, a machine, etc.).

O Use a vertical shot every once in a while instead of the more usual horizontal one to add interest to your page.

O Remove anything that would create a distracting bright spot in the background.

O Use foregrounds and backgrounds (such as foliage or buildings) to add texture.

LIGHTING

Lighting is critical to your photos. Automatic cameras make judgments about exposure for you. With cameras that aren't automatic, however, it's a little more complicated. You have to choose the settings. Whether you're using color or black-and-white film also makes a difference. Here are some general guidelines for taking best advantage of available light, whatever type of film you use:

O Open the curtains, take the shades off the lamps, go outside.

O Schedule shoots for good weather conditions and at the best time of day.

O Make sure that the faces of your subjects are adequately lit.

O Shoot in light shade if the sunlight is bright enough to make your subjects squint.

Remember that time of day and weather conditions can both make a difference. Shoot several rolls of film under a variety of circumstances and see what kind of results you get.

If you have to use a flash, do some experimenting and learn some techniques to keep your photos from looking too stark and unnatural. If your flash is built into the camera, you can cover it with tissue paper or gauze to diffuse the light. If your flash isn't built-in, bounce its light off a wall, a low ceiling, a white curtain, or a tablecloth.

Available light, however, produces the most realistic photos and you should use it whenever possible. If you can see an image, it will register on black-and-white film. I've taken hundreds of mug shots indoors using whatever light was available—daylight from windows, fluorescent lights, and so on—and had perfectly good results. You can get very good results under fluorescent lights with black-and-white film.

Sometimes, however, you may not have enough light indoors for a proper exposure. If you will routinely take photographs in your office building, take a lot of practice shots. Remember to take advantage of the available light by shooting near windows and turning on lights, if necessary.

If you're unsure about light and you have a camera that lets you change the settings, use a technique called *bracketing* (shooting at several different camera settings). To bracket your shots:

1. Take your photos in a range of f-stops around the one indicated—two stops above and two stops below.

2. If you need a certain f-stop to maintain depth of field, shoot with a range of shutter speeds around the one indicated. For instance, if $\frac{1}{125}$ sec is indicated, take one at that speed, then one at $\frac{1}{90}$ sec, and then another at $\frac{1}{200}$ sec.

3. Shoot with a range of ASA settings. For instance, if you're using 200 ASA film, shoot at the correct setting, then shoot at 150 ASA and then at 300 ASA.

4. *Push* your film; that is, shoot at an ASA rating above the rating of the film you're using and then compensate for the change in the developing. For instance, if you're using 400 ASA film, you might shoot the entire roll at 800 ASA or 1600 ASA. Be sure to record the numbers immediately so that you can give the developing service accurate information.

PHOTOGRAPHING PEOPLE

If your newsletter is typical, most of the photographs will be of people. You will no doubt be taking plenty of portraits, people-in-action photos, and group shots.

PORTRAITS.   Portraits, or mug shots, are head-and-shoulder shots of individuals. Here are some simple guidelines to follow:

O Ask your subject to fill his or her cheeks with air and blow it out. (You'll get a more relaxed smile.)

O Shoot a three-quarter view of the shoulders and face rather than a straight-on shot.

O Put more space in front of the subject than behind.

O If your picture includes the torso, make sure that the hands show.

O Have the subject lean forward into the picture.

Generally, a man looks better with his chin tilted slightly up and a woman better with her chin tilted slightly down. Figure 8-1 shows some portraits.

Figure 8-1. Portraits. *Top left*, a casual portrait for an informal occasion. *Top right*, a more formal portrait. *Bottom*, including the subject's environment adds character. (Photos by Patricia Williams.)

Figure 8-2. People-in-action. Add interest to photos by shooting the subject in action in a natural environment. (Photo by Patricia Williams.)

PEOPLE-IN-ACTION PHOTOS.   Photographs are more appealing if you catch the subject in the midst of doing something, rather than posing for the camera. If the president is handing out an anniversary award to an employee, for example, snap the picture just as they shake hands or as they are chatting before the award is made. Try to give photos a personal touch. Capture people in their element to make the pictures alive and interesting as in Figure 8-2.

GROUP SHOTS.   Again, try to capture people in their element. Photograph them in their natural surroundings and, if possible, interacting with each other rather than lined up facing the camera. Ask your subjects to talk to each other or discuss a relevant object of interest. For instance, shoot the planning committee at work while they are talking to each other or examining photographs, papers, plans, or models. Figures 8-3 and 8-4 show examples of group photos.

If you have to shoot a large group, use the bleacher method. The people in the front row sit in chairs, the people in the middle row stand behind them, and the people in the back row stand on chairs.

GETTING FINISHED PRINTS

For predictable results, find a reliable laboratory to develop all of your film. You may want a laboratory that makes halftones and photostats as well. (Chapter 12, "Laying Out and Making Up Pages," discusses halftones and photostats.) Often, if you use a small laboratory, the workers will have the time and motivation to give you some help. Shooting many rolls of film, experimenting, and working with the lab will teach you how to get the results you need.

CUSTOM FINISHING

The laboratory can *push* your film by giving it a longer time in the first development bath or *pull* it by giving it a shorter time. The more a film is pushed, the greater its contrast and the coarser its grain. Pulling, on the other hand, reduces contrast and flattens the image.

Laboratories can also do custom work for you such as dodging, burning, and cropping. *Dodging* withholds light to bring out details in shadows or creates light areas where

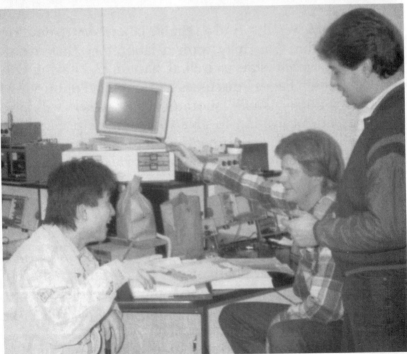

Figure 8-3. Group photos. *Top*, the photo looks unnatural and forced with the two-by-two lineup cutting the picture in half. Also, an antenna seems to be sprouting from the head of the subject second from the right. *Bottom*, this photo is more dynamic; the subjects interact and the shot is composed of curves, not straight lines. (Photos by Patricia Williams.)

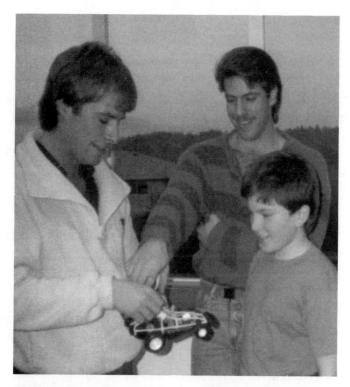

Figure 8-4. Group photos. The interaction of the subjects gives the photo energy. The horizon and the window bars in the background don't cut the picture in half either vertically or horizontally. (Photo by Patricia Williams.)

you can add black type. *Burning* adds light to bring out highlights or to create dark areas where you can add reverse type.

If you have color film that you want to print in black-and-white, take it to a professional laboratory, although you may get muddy looking prints.

CROPPING

You can improve a photo or give it a more dramatic focal point by *cropping* it (eliminating any portions that distract from the main theme). Judicious cropping has boosted the quality of many photos from mediocre to excellent. Use the guidelines listed earlier in the section "Composing Your Photographs." The three most important ones bear repeating:

1. Use only one focal point in your photo.

2. Remember that you want a composition based on thirds, not halves. Watch out for those elements that cut photographs in half either horizontally or vertically.

3. Watch out for series of objects or people in straight lines. Curved lines are easier for the eye to follow.

To help you decide how to crop a photo, see how it would look cropped several different ways. Cut two L-shaped pieces of paper about 10 by 4 inches. Lay them over opposite corners of the photo and adjust the height and width. Remember that although you are fitting the photo to the width of the column, you must also keep the height in mind so that the total composition is pleasing. *Scaling* is the method used for producing the right proportions. You may also need to reduce or enlarge photographs to fit your space. Figure 8-5 shows how cropping can improve a photo.

You can get your photos cropped and sized in two different ways. You can have them cropped and sized when you have the prints made at the photo lab, or later when you order halftones. (Chapter 12, "Laying Out and Making Up Pages," discusses halftones, how to scale, and how to specify new dimensions.)

Figure 8-5. Cropping. *Top*, the original print places the subject in the center of a lot of busy detail. Cropping removes the distracting elements and moves the subject off-center for a more lively picture. (Photo by Patricia Williams.)

HANDLING AND FILING

For convenience in handling, have your negatives printed on *contact sheets* (large sheets that contain small prints of all your shots). Contact sheets are very handy for comparing and choosing which shots you want to print. They're also handy for creating a photo file. Keep the negatives in scratchproof sleeves and staple or tape them to the contact sheet before filing.

The images on the contact sheets are small and you'll need either a magnifying glass or a loupe, which you can buy at an art supply store, to examine them. If, like me, your eyes aren't up to it, you may have to get regular-sized prints as well. Anytime you are cropping photos, you'll need regular-sized prints anyway.

SUMMARY

Photos, more than any other graphic element, give your newsletter vigor, warmth, and human interest. The most important points in this chapter are

1. Tell photographers exactly what you need before sending them to a photo session.

2. Give the photographer a credit line when you print the photo.

3. Label the photos as soon as you get the prints, indicating subject matter, date, and name of the photographer. Use a gummed label rather than writing directly on the back of the photo.

4. When taking photos, move in on the subject and compose your shots by visualizing the picture, using

a focal point, composing the photo in thirds instead of halves, using people as subjects, and removing distracting elements.

5. Get as much light as possible on the face of your subject by opening curtains, shooting outside, and taking shades off lamps.

6. When shooting portraits, shoot a three-quarter rather than a straight-on view, put more space in front of the subject than behind, show the hands if you include the torso, and have the subject lean forward into the picture.

7. Shoot people in action in their natural element for more pleasing and interesting photos.

8. Experiment. Shoot many practice rolls of film.

9. Crop photos to eliminate distracting elements and to give each photo a focal point.

For more information on photography, see the "Resources" section at the end of this book.

Chapter 9 gives an overview of the production process as well as methods of making up pages, composing and outputting type, and creating illustrations.

Choosing
Production Methods

OVERVIEW OF PRINT PRODUCTION

PAGE MAKEUP

TYPE COMPOSITION AND OUTPUT

ILLUSTRATIONS

Phototypesetting? Imagesetting? Paste-up? Desktop publishing? Scanners? Dpi? Welcome to the world of print production with its expanding technology and multitude of choices. You have a very big question to answer: How are you going to produce your newsletter? Whether you're creating a newsletter, or researching a new method of print production, you can use this chapter, which reviews both the traditional and the newer computer-related methods of getting your newsletter ready for print. Chapter 10 discusses your options for printing.

OVERVIEW OF PRINT PRODUCTION

Once, you'd have had no difficulty deciding how to produce your newsletter; the choices were limited. But today, computer technology has, and is, revolutionizing print production and you have a dazzling and somewhat confusing array of methods to choose from. And although the variety of methods available can complicate decision making, the truth is that publishing a quality newsletter has never been easier. Many organizations that are short on money or experience in print production are now able to put out a quality newsletter. Sandra Kurtz, editor of *Northwest DANCE Focus*, says that without computer software her organization wouldn't have a newsletter. "Computer software is simple to use," says Sandra. "It teaches you how to produce a newsletter, even if you have no experience or background in print."

Sandra works on a relatively ancient Macintosh 512E, using MacWrite, a word processing program, to compose the text and the most common desktop publishing program, PageMaker by Aldus, to make up the pages, which she prints out on a laser printer. She then pastes the pages on boards, adds clip art, and ships boards and photos to a quick-print shop.

Sandra's routine is typical for many newsletter editors, but there are other procedures used to produce newsletters. Each procedure, however, includes five basic steps:

1. Compose text and create type.
2. Create illustrations (including photographs).
3. Prepare type and illustrations for printing.
4. Combine type and illustrations on pages ready for reproduction.
5. Reproduce the required number of copies.

There are various options, outlined in Table 9-1, for accomplishing these tasks.

PAGE MAKEUP

How you arrive at camera-ready copy, with text and art integrated, depends on your resources. Today, there are two basic methods of page makeup. You can prepare your

Table 9-1. Options for Accomplishing Production Tasks

Task	Options
Composing text	• Typewriter • Word processing program • Scanning of existing text
Outputting type	• Typewriter • Conventional typesetter • Laser printer • Daisy-wheel printer
Making up pages	• Traditional paste-up • Advanced word processing program • Desktop publishing program
Outputting master pages	• Imagesetter • Laser printer • Dot-matrix printer
Creating illustrations	• Pen and ink • Clip art • Transfer art • Draw or paint program • Computer clip art • Graph or chart programs • Scanning of existing art

pages for print in the traditional way, using adhesive and paste-up boards, or in the new way, using computer technology.

TRADITIONAL LAYOUT AND PASTE-UP

With the conventional method of layout and paste-up, type and illustrations are prepared separately, the pieces are arranged in a layout for each page, and then everything is pasted in place on a board to create a paste-up. A *paste-up*, sometimes called a *mechanical*, is a camera-ready assemblage of all the copy. Figure 9-1 shows a paste-up in progress.

There are several options for composing and outputting type. If you're on a low budget, you can use a typewriter. If you have a personal computer, you can compose the text with a word processing program and output it on a computer printer. If you need high quality, you can have your copy typeset. You'll find a detailed discussion of the options for composing and outputting type later in this chapter. Figure 9-2 illustrates the traditional print production process using typewritten copy, whereas Figure 9-3 illustrates it, using typeset copy.

If you don't want to add a paste-up artist to your staff, you can contract the work out to a graphics service or a free-lance artist. Typesetters and print shops often include layout and paste-up among their services.

It's possible, of course, that you could learn to paste up yourself. The prerequisites are patience and innate neatness. There are some people, however, even some very creative people, who simply cannot produce neat, clean paste-ups.

COMPUTER-BASED PAGE MAKEUP

The other option for making up your pages is to use personal computer technology, which is fast becoming the more common and popular method.

Every personal computer is run by an operating system—a software program that directs the flow of data. Two standard operating systems dominate the industry, MS-DOS, which is used on IBM and IBM-compatible computers, and Apple's proprietary Macintosh system. Although other manufacturers with proprietary operating

Figure 9-1. Traditional paste-up in progress

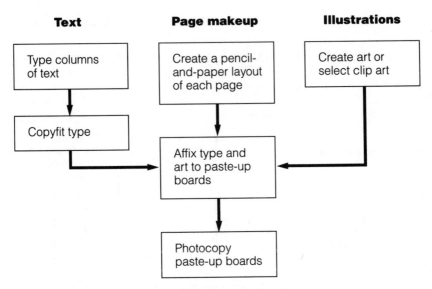

Figure 9-2. Traditional page makeup, typewriter. If you compose your text with a typewriter and then affix the text and illustrations to a board to create a paste-up, you're using an old but honorable method.

systems are entering the field, the software and equipment available for publishing a newsletter right now are either MS-DOS or Macintosh oriented.

If your organization has one of these computers, you can use either a desktop publishing or a word processing program to make up the pages (sometimes called master pages) of your newsletter. Figure 9-4 shows a paste-up in progress in a desktop publishing program.

Computer technology is expanding rapidly and every day more and more manufacturers introduce products to make newsletter production easier and better. Jeremy Robkin, who operates InnoVisions Creative Services, strongly believes that you can achieve professional-looking results with desktop publishing and that the days when it was considered an alternative for amateurs are far behind.

Figure 9-3. Traditional page makeup, typesetting. The traditional method, made easier with computer technology, still produces the highest print quality. The steps in the process can vary, of course. You might use original pen-and-ink drawings, for instance, or deliver text files by disk.

Several publications are devoted to desktop publishing and a periodic scan of their articles and advertisements can keep you up-to-date on what is available. (See the "Resources" section at the end of this book.)

DESKTOP PUBLISHING PROGRAMS. Desktop publishing programs are page makeup programs that let you design and lay out your pages right on the computer screen. Al-

Figure 9-4. Paste-up in progress in a desktop publishing program. Paste-up is being created with Aldus's PageMaker program. (Courtesy of the Raima Corporation and InnoVisions Creative Services.)

dus's PageMaker and Xerox's Ventura Publisher are the two major names in desktop publishing. You compose the text with a word processing program, create the illustrations with a paint or draw program, and then import both text and art into the desktop publishing program. Then you're able to lay out your pages right on the computer screen. Figure 9-5 shows a typical print production process, using a desktop publishing program.

Recent versions of these programs also give you the choice of creating the text and graphics directly, but this is not a serious option at present. Today, many people combine traditional methods with computer technology. For instance, they use computer programs to compose the text, create some illustrations, and produce master pages. They then paste on clip art or other pen-and-ink drawings in the old way. The process you use, if you decide to use computer technology, will be one that you develop to suit your needs.

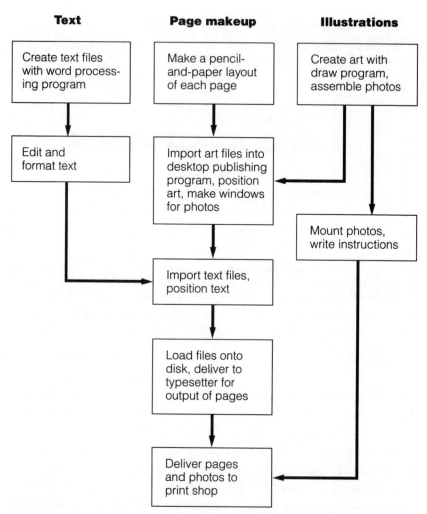

Figure 9-5. Page makeup with a desktop publishing program. Using word processing and desktop publishing programs, you save time and money by doing most of the work on the computer screen and still get professional-looking results. You can vary the process according to your needs. For instance, you might scan the photos and the art and include them in your pages right on the computer screen.

If you want to include photographs in your newsletter, you have to convert them into *halftones* (reproductions of photos or other continuous-image illustrations created with a multitude of dark, dense dots). In desktop publishing, you have two options. You can have halftones made in the traditional way with a process camera. Or, you can use a scanner to digitize the photo so that the desktop publishing software can read it. Although scanner technology is improving, the resolution in the final printed image won't be as good as the resolution obtained with the traditional method.

It's hard to keep up with the innovations. If you want to print in color, equipment for color separations is available. You can even go directly from the desktop publishing program to the printing press, eliminating many of the tedious steps in-between.

WORD PROCESSING PROGRAMS. One advance in technology that is exciting to newsletter publishers is the page makeup capabilities offered in the latest versions of Microsoft Word and WordPerfect. More software companies will soon follow suit no doubt. With these programs, you can now create columns, integrate illustrations onto the page, wrap text around illustrations, and then preview the pages before you print them out. Figure 9-6 shows page makeup in a word processing program.

This method is less expensive than desktop publishing and some authorities on computer publishing technology consider these programs a viable alternative to desktop publishing. You have the same options for adding photos that you do with desktop publishing. Figure 9-7 illustrates a typical print production process using a word processing program. However, if you need great flexibility in page layout and typographical control, you'll find it in a desktop publishing system.

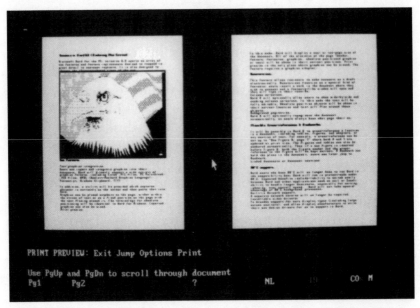

Figure 9-6. Screen showing a paste-up in progress in Microsoft Word. (Courtesy of Microsoft Word.)

TYPE COMPOSITION AND OUTPUT

The type in your newsletter falls into two categories: *body copy*, the text of your stories, and *headlines*, the copy set in larger or display-size type to attract attention. In this book, captions for illustrations are included as part of the body copy.

The list on page 158 shows the options for composing and outputting body-copy type for traditional paste-ups.

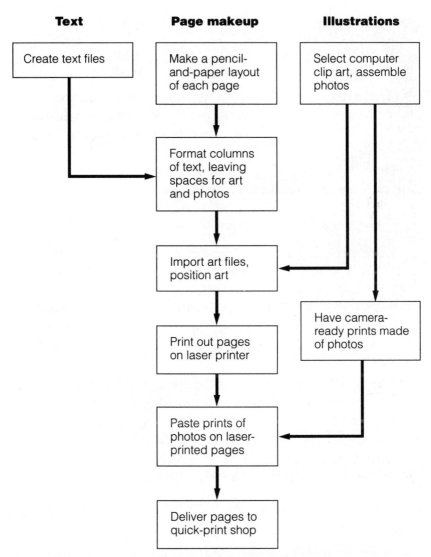

Figure 9-7. Page makeup with a word processing program. If you use a word processing program with page makeup capabilities, like the newest versions of Microsoft Word and WordPerfect, you can lay out your pages right on the computer screen. You have other options for several of the steps, of course. For instance, instead of using computer clip art, you might add transfer art or traditional clip art to the laser-printed pages.

COMPOSITION	*OUTPUT*
Word processing	Galleys of phototypeset columns Laser-printed columns
Typewriter	Typewritten columns of text Galleys of phototypeset columns (scanned from typewritten text)

Here are the major options for composing and outputting type already made up into pages.

COMPOSITION	*OUTPUT*
Word processing	Laser-printed pages (via either word processing or desktop publishing) Imageset pages (by typesetting equipment geared to desktop publishing)

The type output by these different systems varies in quality measured by the *resolution* (degree of fine detail) they offer. Resolution is measured in *dpi* (dots per inch), the more dpi the better the resolution. So that you can compare these options, Figures 9-8 through 9-11 show examples of type output by the various methods.

WORD PROCESSING AND OTHER COMPUTER-RELATED METHODS

You can compose text using a personal computer and a word processing program; a stand-alone, dedicated word processor; or a dedicated publishing system. Word processing on a personal computer is the most common method by far.

Financial counselors say that, as a minimum, you should have six months take-home salary or wages in a savings account as a fund for emergencies. Once you have reached that objective, your savings goal must depend on your family situation, your plans and ambitions, and of course on your income.

Financial counselors say that, as a minimum, you should have six months take-home salary or wages in a savings account as a fund for emergencies. Once you have reached that objective, your savings goal must depend on your family situation, your plans and ambitions, and of course on your income.

Figure 9-8. Examples of type output. *Top,* electric typewriter. *Bottom,* phototypeset output.

Depending on your equipment, you can create text files by

○ keying in the text

○ importing existing text files by telecommunications

○ loading a disk containing existing text files

○ reading existing copy into the computer with a scanner

Financial counselors say that, as a minimum, you should have six months take-home salary or wages in a savings account as a fund for emergencies. Once you have reached that objective, your savings goal must depend on your family situation, your plans and ambitions, and of course on your income.

Financial counselors say that, as a minimum, you should have six months take-home salary or wages in a savings account as a fund for emergencies. Once you have reached that objective, your savings goal must depend on your family situation, your plans and ambitions, and of course on your income.

Financial counselors say that, as a minimum, you should have six months take-home salary or wages in a savings account as a fund for emergencies. Once you have reached that objective, your savings goal must depend on your family situation, your plans and ambitions, and of course on your income.

Figure 9-9. Examples of computer printer output. *Top,* daisy-wheel printer. *Middle,* dot-matrix printer (near-letter quality). *Bottom,* laser printer, output in columns for paste-up.

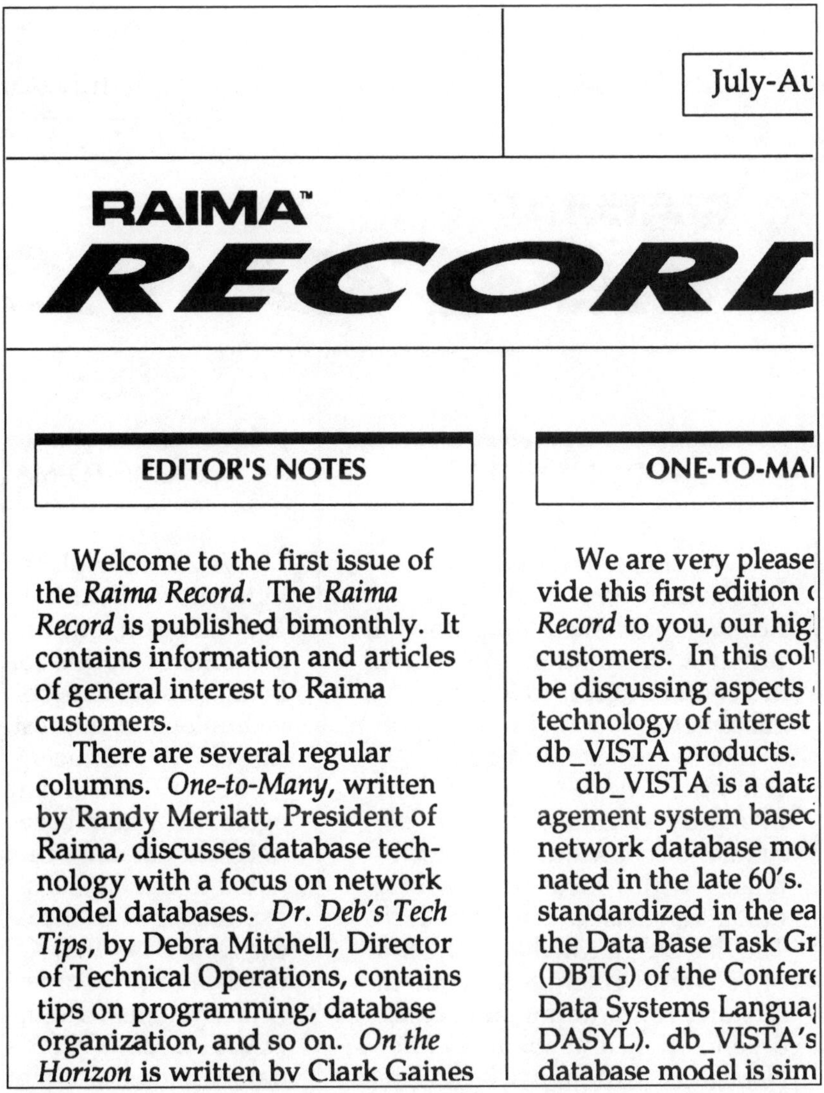

July-Au

RAIMA™

RECORD

EDITOR'S NOTES

ONE-TO-MAI

Welcome to the first issue of the *Raima Record*. The *Raima Record* is published bimonthly. It contains information and articles of general interest to Raima customers.

There are several regular columns. *One-to-Many*, written by Randy Merilatt, President of Raima, discusses database technology with a focus on network model databases. *Dr. Deb's Tech Tips*, by Debra Mitchell, Director of Technical Operations, contains tips on programming, database organization, and so on. *On the Horizon* is written by Clark Gaines

We are very please vide this first edition c *Record* to you, our hig customers. In this col be discussing aspects technology of interest db_VISTA products.

db_VISTA is a data agement system based network database moc nated in the late 60's. standardized in the ea the Data Base Task Gr (DBTG) of the Confere Data Systems Langua; DASYL). db_VISTA's database model is sim

Figure 9-10. Laser printer output. This page was composed with a desktop publishing program and output by a laser printer at 300 dpi. (Courtesy of the Raima Corporation and InnoVisions Creative Services.)

July-Au

RAIMA™

RECORD

EDITOR'S NOTES

ONE-TO-MAN

Welcome to the first issue of
the *Raima Record*. The *Raima
Record* is published bimonthly. It
contains information and articles
of general interest to Raima
customers.

There are several regular
columns. *One-to-Many*, written
by Randy Merilatt, President of
Raima, discusses database technology with a focus on network
model databases. *Dr. Deb's Tech
Tips*, by Debra Mitchell, Director
of Technical Operations, contains
tips on programming, database
organization, and so on. *On the
Horizon* is written by Clark Gaines

We are very please
vide this first edition o
Record to you, our higl
customers. In this col
be discussing aspects o
technology of interest
db_VISTA products.

db_VISTA is a data
agement system based
network database mod
nated in the late 60's.
standardized in the ea
the Data Base Task Gr
(DBTG) of the Confere
Data Systems Languag
DASYL). db_VISTA's
database model is sim

Figure 9-11. Example of imagesetting output. This page was composed
with a desktop publishing program and output by imagesetting at 1,270 dpi.
(Courtesy of the Raima Corporation and InnoVisions Creative Services.)

WORD PROCESSING PROGRAMS. The major word processing programs available today, such as Microsoft Word
and WordPerfect are very sophisticated, offering not only
the page makeup capabilities discussed previously, but also
spelling and grammar checkers, thesauri, and outlining
and indexing utilities.

When you compose your text with a word processing
program, your choices for output are

- O phototypesetter
- O imagesetter (pages composed with a desktop
  publishing program)
- O commercial laser printer
- O inhouse laser printer
- O inhouse daisy-wheel or dot-matrix printer (used
  mostly to produce drafts)

With the first three options, you can deliver text files by disk
or by telecommunications to a commercial typesetter.

You can also use a word processing program as part of
an inhouse publishing system (see the section on dedicated
systems).

DEDICATED WORD PROCESSORS. Dedicated (stand-alone)
word processors—made by companies like Lanier, Xerox,
and Wang—are big investments. If your organization already has this type of equipment, including a letter-quality
printer, you know that it produces crisp, clean-looking
type. Most machines also offer a variety of type styles.

If, however, you want to send the copy to be typeset, a
dedicated word processor would probably not be a good
choice. They usually have idiosyncratic disk formats and
coding systems and the files require conversion, which adds
time, money, and frustration to the production process.

DEDICATED PUBLISHING SYSTEMS.   Some companies have serious computer equipment like a mainframe or a network of minicomputers with powerful publishing facilities, including typesetting equipment. Typically, you use a text editor to create text files, inserting formatting codes directly into the text. You can then transmit the text files electronically to a photocopy machine, a computer page printer, or a phototypesetting machine. You can also use your word processing program and a typesetter interface to format and send files to phototypesetting equipment. These systems are very expensive, require more training, and are less attractive now that personal computer systems are offering better and more sophisticated facilities.

SCANNERS.   Another option for composing text is a *scanner*, a device that "reads" and digitizes existing text, illustrations, and photos and imports them into a computer program. Many scanners look like small photocopiers, with a flat glass platen on which you place the page you want to scan.

In "reading" text, the machine scans the page and digitizes the characters, then optical character recognition (OCR) software stores the characters in the ASCII format so that the text can be accessed by a word processing program. A scanner cannot read everything. Most OCR software will recognize only ten or twelve common typefaces, although some can be trained to read additional ones. Some OCR programs also include formatting such as underlining and paragraph indenting. Most scanners offer a resolution of 300 dots per inch (dpi)—to match typical laser printer resolution—but some recent manufacturers now advertise 400 dpi. Your computer must be compatible with and have adequate memory for your model of scanner.

Scanners can be very expensive. Instead of buying a scanner, you can take your copy to a print shop or a typesetter for conversion by commercial scanning equipment.

PHOTOTYPESET OUTPUT

Phototypesetting outputs the crispest, most professional looking text because you get

○ resolution at 1200 lines per inch, typically, although commercial typesetters can go much higher

○ proportional spacing that saves space and is easier to read

○ very clear and sharp characters

○ uniform spacing and straight lines

○ a large variety of type styles and sizes

○ flexibility in spacing, alignment, and justification

Phototypesetting is a term that covers photomechanical, digitized cathode ray tube (CRT), and digitized laser type-setting equipment. Although they are all phototypesetters, they differ in their method of image formation. Alistair Campbell in his book *The Graphic Designer's Handbook* offers the clearest and briefest description:

> The photomechanical method produces typeset matter ("output") by light being shone through a film negative of the typeform onto photographic film or paper. Digitized CRT produces output either by a contact process—film or paper is placed over the front of the CRT itself (onto which the image is projected through a system of fibre optics)—or by optical transmission of the tube beams directly onto photographic film or paper. Thirdly, digitized lasers, as the name suggests, use a laser instead of a CRT to produce the image.

Digitized laser typesetting is the latest innovation. Digitized CRT is still very common. Photomechanical typesetting is on the way out.

TRADITIONAL OUTPUT.   In traditional phototypesetting, you typically deliver a disk containing your text files to the typesetter. Sometimes you also include typewritten or word-processed copy, with instructions marked on it. You might also be able to transmit the files by telecommunications, if you and the typesetter have compatible equipment.

Another option, if the typesetter has a scanner, is to deliver only typed or word-processed copy. What you want to avoid is having the typesetter key in the text again, since the extra step in the process costs you time and money.

Talk to the typesetter about what forms of copy are acceptable. Discuss hardware and software compatibility. Text files created by word processing programs may have formatting codes that will have to be either replaced or translated in the typesetting process. And, if you are sending typed copy, ask the typesetter how to mark instructions on it.

The phototypeset output you receive will be in *galleys* (type set in columns on glossy paper) ready for you to trim and add to your paste-up.

Generally, unless you're publishing a slick newsletter with wide distribution, you're better off using a small company that will appreciate your business. Often, you can have typesetting, paste-up, and printing done by the same shop.

Remember, typesetting is more time-consuming and more expensive than the other methods. If you need a professional look and can afford it, typesetting can't be beat. On the other hand, if you neither need nor want a polished, expensive look in your newsletter, one of the other methods would probably fit your image better.

IMAGESETTING OUTPUT.   The rapid advance of page makeup and desktop publishing technology has given rise to typesetting equipment called imagesetters, which typically produce output with a resolution of 1,270 or 1,693 dpi. The shops that provide imagesetting services are often called service bureaus.

You compose your pages, including illustrations, with a desktop publishing program, load the files onto a disk, and take it to the shop. The shop produces master pages on glossy paper (or on film) that are ready for printing. Before final output of type, however, the typesetter can print galley proofs on a laser printer for you.

Because Linotype's Linotronic equipment has dominated imagesetting, people often say that they're taking the newsletter down to be "linotronned." However, other manufacturers, most notably CompuGraphic, have entered the market with competitive equipment.

Most of the service bureaus are Macintosh-oriented, although some do accept MS-DOS (the standard operating system for IBM and IBM clones) files and translate them into a form they can use. The extra step adds to the cost, of course. As MS-DOS gains on Macintosh in offering page composition packages, however, more and more service bureaus will be able to accept MS-DOS files. The big name in desktop publishing software—Aldus's PageMaker—has packages for both systems. Xerox's Ventura Publisher is MS-DOS only, although a Macintosh program is in the works. Several other software packages are only for the Macintosh.

COMPUTER-PRINTER OUTPUT

Another alternative for outputting type is a computer printer, most notably a laser printer. If you're producing a low-budget newsletter or you need the friendly casual look, you might also consider a dot-matrix or daisy-wheel printer. Although the resolution with computer printer output is not as good as that from phototypesetting, it can be improved. Have camera-ready prints (called photostats or veloxes) made of the copy, reducing it to 85–90 percent of its original size. This extra step does add to your costs.

LASER PRINTERS.   A laser printer produces the best resolution of all computer printers and, if you need higher quality, it's the only printer suitable for producing master pages. Typically, laser printers offer a resolution of 300 dpi (remember, a phototypesetter produces 1,200 dots per inch and more). More expensive models offer 400 dpi and even better resolution is on the way.

The technology is similar to that used in photocopy machines because, although the images are created digitally by computer codes, they are formed with toner. A laser printer prints graphics as well as text. Some laser printers can also print in color.

Laser printers are fast and, although expensive, their price is coming down. Instead of purchasing equipment, you may want to send your copy to one of the many small firms that offer laser printing.

There are two types of laser printers: those that can read PostScript files and those that cannot. Adobe's PostScript is a *page description language (PDL)* that gives instructions to the printer. It's the industry standard, available on many laser printers and also on several models of imagesetting typesetters from Linotype. An MS-DOS system will support both types of printers, but if you have Macintosh-compatible page makeup software, you have to have a PostScript printer.

Laser printers come equipped with resident (built-in) fonts. If you have one of the more powerful printers, you can also use software to download what are called soft fonts into the printer's memory. Then, depending on the size of your printer's memory, you can use two or more fonts in a single document. Some printers also have slots so that you can add cartridges containing additional fonts.

DOT-MATRIX PRINTERS.   Although they do print graphics as well as text, dot-matrix printers are best suited for printing drafts, not for producing master pages. Characters are composed of dots formed by impact on the paper through an inked film or plastic ribbon. The more pins a dot-matrix printer has on its printing head, the more dots per inch and the better the quality. The number of pins in the print head can range from nine to twenty-four.

You can print denser characters with most dot-matrix printers by choosing a bold or near-letter-quality option. The type wheel moves back and forth across the paper as it imprints and produces heavier or bolder inking by making multiple passes. However, multiple passes slow the process down considerably. Typically, the resolution is only 180 dpi. You can buy software that will enhance the output to get better results.

Each printer comes equipped with its own standard fonts, usually a variety of sizes in one type style. You can purchase software to create additional fonts.

A dot-matrix printer is faster than a daisy-wheel printer but if you use software to enhance the quality of the text or create fonts, you will lengthen the time spent printing.

DAISY-WHEEL PRINTERS.   Daisy-wheel printers produce what is called letter-quality text, better quality than that produced by a dot-matrix printer. The type is similar in appearance and quality to type produced by an electric typewriter. Daisy-wheel printers do not, however, print graphics.

The daisy wheels are interchangeable metal wheels, each one holding a font of type. They produce the type by impact on an inked ribbon made of film. Because you have to change daisy wheels manually, it's difficult to change typefaces and type sizes. Compared to other printers, daisy-wheel printers are slow.

TYPEWRITER AND DIRECT-IMPRESSION TYPESETTING

Typewriters have and are producing a lot of fine newsletters and, although direct-impression typesetters are almost obsolete, some companies still own and use them.

TYPEWRITER.   If your budget is small, you can produce your copy on a typewriter. The conventional wisdom is that an IBM Executive or an IBM Selectric creates the best-looking type. With the IBM Selectric, for instance, you can choose from a number of type styles. Most typewriters use *monospacing* (each character sits in a space that's the same size as every other character). A few models do offer a system of modified proportional spacing that, for some purposes, makes for a more attractive newsletter.

You can improve the resolution of typewritten copy by reducing it to 80 percent of its original size. This means a little extra trouble because you have to lay out pages that are 125 percent as large as the desired size. It's also extremely hard to justify the text in a typewritten column and usually not worth the effort. These two facts may be drawbacks or they may not. The typewriter look is a traditional one for newsletters and it may be just what you want.

If you do take typewritten copy to a phototypesetter, look for one that can scan your copy. If the typesetter has to key it in, your costs will go up.

DIRECT-IMPRESSION TYPESETTING.   A direct-impression typesetter (sometimes called "strike on") is like a large typewriter. If your company owns one, it's probably an IBM Selectric Composer. If any small type shops still use this type of equipment, I haven't been able to find one.

A direct-impression typesetter offers some features of real typesetting, such as proportional spacing and a wide selection of type styles and sizes, plus it's relatively easy to use. As with a typewriter, the biggest problem is producing error-free copy. When you make typing mistakes, you have to either retype the copy or make corrections with liquid white-out or white correction tape.

Maintenance and repairs present another difficulty. Because direct-impression typesetters are no longer being manufactured, parts are hard to find and repairs are almost impossible. If the machine quits, you may have to find another means to produce your type in a hurry.

HEADLINE TYPE

Type for headlines and subheads ranges in size from 14 points to 36 points. If you have your newsletter typeset commercially, you simply specify the type style and size for your headlines along with the body copy. If you use word processing or desktop publishing software, you can produce headlines with font programs, or with paint or draw programs. Transfer lettering and headline machines are other options.

TRANSFER LETTERING. The letters are imprinted on sheets of plastic that you can buy in art or office supply stores. You then rub the letters onto the paste-up board with a dull pencil point or other smooth instrument. Large letters are easier to apply than small ones.

HEADLINING MACHINES. Headlining machines are compact little machines that produce nothing but characters for headlines, displays, artwork, and overheads. They offer a range of type styles and sizes suitable for newsletters. Many of these machines are operated by hand and produce one letter at a time. The type comes out on plastic tape that can then be used for paste-up. Other machines, such as the Kroy 190 Lettering System, have keyboards and allow text to be previewed and corrected before being printed.

The graphics departments of many large companies include headlining machines among their equipment. If your company doesn't own one, or if you don't want to purchase one, you should be able to find one at a print or type shop.

ILLUSTRATIONS

The options for creating illustrations—drawings, lines, screens, symbols, and ornaments—are many. You can, of course, have an artist create original art for your newsletter, but most art for newsletters comes from clip art, transfer sheets, or computer paint or draw programs. Most newsletters also include photographs among their illustrations.

CLIP ART

The variety of graphics—including illustrations, lines, letters, and symbols—that you can obtain with this method is staggering. You can find books containing collections of clip art in office, stationery, and art supply stores. These books contain art suitable for every purpose including holidays and sporting and other special events. You can find a variety of borders, ornaments, and design motifs such as Grecian, art deco, art nouveau, and Victorian. You might also be able to find hard-cover books of clip art at your local bookstore. Check their bargain tables every once in a while. And you might subscribe to one of the clip art services that will mail you a book of new clip art, timed for seasonal and holiday use, at regular intervals. Figure 9-12 shows examples of clip art. Typesetters and printers may also have

Figure 9-12. Clip art. These examples were clipped from clip art books produced by Graphics Products Corporation.

books of design that contain material that you can reproduce. Look at the ads in your telephone book's yellow pages for companies that advertise this service.

TRANSFER ART

Another source for graphics is transfer art. Like transfer lettering, the images are on plastic sheets and you rub them off onto your paste-up board or your master page. Transfer art is also available from art supply stores, stationery stores, and some office supply stores.

Transfer art includes alphabets of beautifully designed characters; borders and rules; design elements such as dots, blocks, and stars; and symbols used in professions such as architecture and engineering. Some of the common brands are Chartpak, Letraset, and Formatt. Figure 9-13 shows examples of transfer art.

COMPUTER ART

Computer programs can also produce all kinds of drawings, illustrations, graphs and charts, and designs. If you want to produce art to import into a word processing or page makeup program, you have to make sure all the software is compatible. More and more of these products come on the market every day.

GRAPH AND CHART PROGRAMS. You can find a great many programs to help you produce graphs and charts that interpret data in numeric form. The program you choose should offer a wide range of styles and be easy to use. Figure 9-14 shows examples of graphs and charts created with computer programs.

PAINT AND DRAW PROGRAMS. Freehand drawing programs are usually called *paint* programs. You can draw illustrations freehand, but you can also choose from a variety

Figure 9-13. Transfer art. These examples of illustrations, borders, letters, and symbols were taken from sheets of transfer art produced by Chartpak and DECAdry.

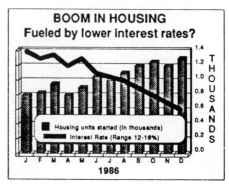

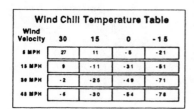

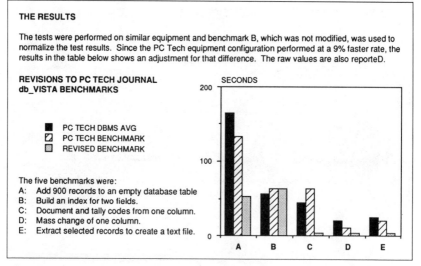

Figure 9-14. Computer-produced graphs, charts, and tables. The table, *top left*, is produced with GEM WordChart; the chart, *top right*, with GEM Graph; and the chart, *bottom*, with CricketGraph. (Top table and chart, courtesy of Logitech. Bottom chart courtesy of the Raima Corporation and InnoVisions Creative Services.)

of shapes, patterns, and line thicknesses. Creating art with a paint program can be a little tricky; they're good for producing informal illustrations but, unless you have artistic skills, you shouldn't depend on a paint program for a steady supply of graphics. However, you can buy clip art

Figure 9-15. Art produced with paint and draw programs. *Clockwise, beginning top left*, drawing of man created with Microsoft Paintbrush, owl with GEM Paint, cylinder with SuperPaint, and building with GEM Draw Plus. (Drawings of the owl and the building, courtesy of Digital Research Inc.)

libraries, which contain a variety of art already created for your use.

Drawing programs are good for producing stylized drawings, technical illustrations, and flow and organization charts. You don't have to have artistic skill to produce good results. You can also purchase libraries of predrawn illustrations and assorted shapes. Figure 9-15 shows examples of art produced with paint and draw programs and Figure 9-16 shows examples of computer clip art.

Figure 9-16. Computer clip art. (Courtesy of Metro ImageBase.)

SCANNED ILLUSTRATIONS.   A scanner reads existing draw-ings and photographs in the same way it reads text. Some scanners come with software that allows you to enlarge, shrink, or rotate the images. You may also be able to scan images directly into popular draw or paint programs where you can then edit them on a dot-by-dot basis.

For a photograph or other continuous-image graphic, the image you get for reproduction will not be as sharp as from a halftone produced by a camera. A halftone, as you remember, is a reproduction of a photo or other continu-ous-image illustration made with a multitude of dark, dense dots. The gray-tone gradations in a traditional half-tone are made up of many sizes of dots, with differing densities. The gray-tone gradations produced by scanners, on the other hand, are made up of dots that are all the same size. Figure 9-17 shows an example of a scanned photo, Figure 9-18, a scanned drawing.

Scanner technology is constantly improving. Manufac-turers now advertise gray-scale scanning products—scan-ners, editing software, and printing devices—that make scanning a desirable alternative. If you don't want to invest in this type of equipment, many firms offer commercial scanning services.

Scanners are just one of many exciting technological developments in the area of print production that you may want to research.

THE COM

BUSIN

Report

Volume 1; No. 1

Desktop
Its Sh

Employees
Own Des

Projected Mark

A Clear Prefe

GEM Desktop Publisher Sets Price/Performance Benchmark for Software Industry

Digital Research announces its high performance easy to use, full-function page composition software application -**GEM Desktop Publisher**. Introducing the true price/performer, available at the end of May, at a suggested retail price of $395

"As a product offering, thing that ever happene computers." says deskto

Figure 9-17. Scanner-produced halftone. The halftone was produced by scanning a photo at 300 dpi. The page was composed with GEM Desktop Publisher and output on a laser printer. (Courtesy of Digital Research Inc.)

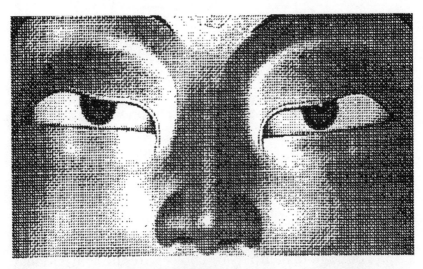

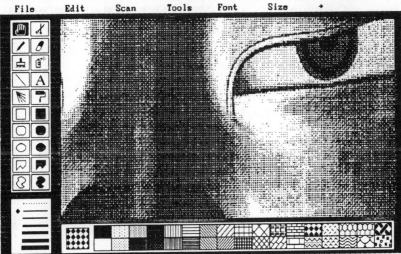

Figure 9-18. Scanner-produced illustration. The illustration was produced by scanning a piece of existing art with ScanMan℗, an inexpensive handheld scanner produced by Logitech. The top image is composed of 200 dpi, increased to 400 dpi in the screen (PaintShow℗ Plus) at bottom. (Courtesy of Logitech.)

SUMMARY

Some advance knowledge of production methods helps as you research the best methods for producing your newsletter. The important points in this chapter are

1. You can now choose between conventional methods of print production and computer-based methods.

2. For outputting type, your choices are the typewriter, a computer with word processing software and a laser printer, or conventional typesetting.

3. For page makeup, your choices are the conventional method, where you paste up text and graphics on a paste-up board; the computer-based method, where you use page makeup software; or a method that's a combination of the two.

4. For illustrations, your choices are original art, clip art, transfer art, or, if you're using a computer, computer-generated art.

5. You should research production methods thoroughly before making your choices. Talk to other people who are producing newsletters about their production methods. Talk to printers, typesetters, and desktop publishing firms.

Chapter 10 gives an overview of printing methods.

CHAPTER **10**

Deciding How to Print Your Newsletter

OFFSET

PHOTOCOPY

MIMEOGRAPH (ELECTRONIC STENCIL
DUPLICATING)

183

Before you choose a method for printing your newsletter, you need answers to the following questions: How much money do you want to spend? Do you need a slick, professional newsletter or a casual, intimate one? What kind of equipment do you have inhouse? How fast do you need the job done?

Read on to find out about the three major options for printing: offset, photocopy, and mimeograph.

OFFSET

Offset is the printing process most widely used today. Briefly, offset works like this: Using a photographic process, the printer makes printing plates from your paste-ups. Depending on the type of press, the process may include making film negatives. Each plate goes onto the printing press, which uses chemical means to ink only the image areas of the plate. The press then prints the images onto the paper that runs through it.

Offset printing offers the highest quality printing. Your text will be sharp and clear, the pages aligned, and the color vivid and in place. Offset printing is usually the most costly method of printing and always the most time-consuming.

If you don't have an inhouse print shop, you can choose between a quick-print shop and a commercial printer. Generally, if you need less than 2,000 copies of each issue, you'll get a better price at a quick-print shop. If you need between 2,000 and 3,000 copies, it's a toss-up. If you print over 3,000, you may get a better price with the commercial printer.

QUICK-PRINT SHOPS

A quick-print shop typically has a smaller press and uses a paper or plastic master for a short run (3,000–4,000 copies). The printer makes plates directly from your camera-ready paste-up, so either you or the printer must paste the halftones on before printing. The shop does fast work, uses standard paper stocks, and can do a limited number of folds. Most inhouse print shops are similar to a quick-print shop.

You'll probably get photocopies of the pages to proof, or a press proof, which means that you must be there when the first sheets are run. Unless you want to turn out a slick professional newsletter with fine screens and perfect color registration, a quick-print shop should do a good job for you.

COMMERCIAL PRINTERS

A commercial printer has a larger press (or presses) and uses more sophisticated technology to produce good-quality copies and a long run. A commercial printer uses a different process to make plates than a quick printer. The plates are made by first producing film negatives of the paste-ups and then stripping in the halftone negatives.

If you use a commercial printer, you have a better choice of paper stocks and folds. The commercial printer also does a superior job of printing photos. However, your turn-around time will probably be longer.

A commercial printer will give you a press proof, or a *blueline* (a contact print), to check before beginning the print run. If your newsletter uses more complex graphic techniques like halftones, screens, or reverse images, you'll need a blueline.

SELECTING A PRINTER

To choose a printer, ask for recommendations from other newsletter editors or from anyone else involved in producing printed materials. When you have three or four possibilities, check each one out, taking along a dummy of your newsletter and its specifications (discussed in Chapter 11, "Designing Your Newsletter"). Discuss the range of services the printer offers, paper stock, and the demands of your time schedule.

ASSESSING PRINT QUALITY.   Ask to look at print samples. Some quick-print shops specialize in "fast-and-dirty" work where speed, not quality, is of primary importance. When assessing the quality of printed materials, check the following points.

- O Photos should be neither too muddy nor too light.
- O There should be no smudges, flaws, or broken letters.
- O Screens should be *registered* properly. (To be in register means to be accurately positioned.)
- O Ink coverage should be consistent and neither too heavy nor too light.

O Ink coverage should be the same on each page.

O Pages should be lined up at the top, with proper margins at right, left, top, bottom, and gutter.

O Trimming should be neat and properly positioned.

O Folds should be in the right place.

To check proofs of your own newsletter, use the procedure above and also check to see that:

O Pages are in the right sequence.

O Graphics are in the right position, scaled and cropped properly, and facing the right direction.

GETTING BIDS. Get bids from at least three printers. To estimate printing costs, a printer needs the following information:

1. name of the newsletter

2. name of the editor

3. date you need the estimate by

4. newsletter specifications

    O paper stock, quality, and weight
    O trim size
    O printed one side or both
    O ink colors
    O number of pages per issue
    O number of copies per issue
    O number of issues per year
    O descriptions of halftones and screens
    O binding, drilling, and folding requirements

You should ask the printer to include the following information in the bid:

1. cost per issue
2. cost per year
3. payment terms

Many experts on print production recommend that you ask for a guaranteed price for a specified period, such as a year or more. Because the price of paper keeps going up, the printer may give you the guarantee, but stipulate that if the price of paper goes up, the price of printing goes up too.

PHOTOCOPY

A good photocopy machine can produce clear and readable copies inexpensively and without too much trouble. A photocopy machine places electrostatic charges in the images of the type and graphics onto either a belt or a drum. A powdered toner sticks to the image areas. When the paper comes into contact with the toner, the images are transferred onto the paper and fused with heat.

Photocopying doesn't give you the quality in reproduction that offset printing or even laser printing does, but it is less expensive and much faster. In addition, photocopy machines are widely available. Most quick-print shops have them and will do the copying for you. Or, you may already have one in your office that you can use.

If you want to include a photograph, you can make a halftone using the photocopy machine and a white-dot screen, available at most art or office supply stores. Place the screen between the photo and the glass on the machine and make the copy. Then add the halftone to your paste-up.

Many of today's photocopy machines are sophisticated and versatile. Some photocopy machines reduce and enlarge, some collate and staple, and some print on both sides. Most photocopiers handle any grade or weight of paper and any surface except gloss coated. Because some photocopy machines also print with color, you could even use a second color in your nameplate and print a supply of newsletter stock ahead of time.

With photocopy, you're limited to the size of paper the machine will handle. You also have to take extra care with your originals; they have to be very clean, with everything pasted down as flat as possible. If you have shadow lines where copy is pasted on, you'll have to cover the cutlines with white correction fluid.

If you have a photocopy machine in your office, you may have to reserve time for your print runs. And, if the machine gets a lot of use, it may be out of action part of the time waiting for service.

Most quick-print shops also do photocopying and they usually have high-quality, sophisticated equipment.

MIMEOGRAPH (ELECTRONIC STENCIL DUPLICATING)

Mimeographing has come a long way from the troublesome days of difficult corrections and smudged ink. In fact, now the machines are usually called electronic stencil duplicators, not mimeographs. With the new equipment, stencils are produced electronically with a stencil scanner and then the stencil is mimeographed with an electronic mess-free stencil duplicator.

A stencil scanner works like a photocopy machine and will reproduce images of text, illustrations, and photographs. Stencil duplicators are also available that print in colors.

Stencil duplicating is the least expensive option. If you're buying equipment, stencil duplicating equipment costs less than a photocopy machine. And, because the paper is less expensive than photocopy paper, the cost per copy is also cheaper. It's also faster than photocopying.

If you don't purchase your own equipment, it may be hard to find a company that cuts and duplicates stencils. It is generally believed that photocopying gives better quality reproduction. However, the manufacturers of electronic stencil equipment claim that only offset printing gives better results.

SUMMARY

The method of printing you choose depends on the type of newsletter you're publishing, your budget, your other resources, and time considerations. The important points in this chapter are

1. Offset printing offers vivid, sharp reproduction. It is the most expensive and time-consuming method. You can use either a quick-print shop or, for a slick and professional look, a commercial printer.

2. If you choose offset printing, get bids from at least three printers, and ask to see samples of their work.

3. Photocopying your newsletter is inexpensive and convenient. Photocopy technology is improving rapidly, offering better quality, back-and-front printing, and colors.

4. Mimeograph (electronic stencil duplicating) has greatly improved technology and is not as messy as

it once was. However, you would probably need to purchase the equipment, because mimeograph shops are not easy to find.

Now that you're familiar with production and print methods, you're ready for Chapter 11, which gives guidelines to help you design your newsletter.

Designing Your Newsletter

DESIGNING THE ELEMENTS

EXAMPLES OF NEWSLETTER DESIGN

The name of a newsletter, its content, and its design all work to project your organization's image, but the design carries the heaviest load. Whether you hire a professional graphics designer or design it yourself, you want your newsletter to be easy to read, appealing, and suitable for your organization's image.

If you decide to hire a professional designer, shop around. If your organization is large, talk to any other employees who produce publications. Ask printers for recommendations. If you have seen a newsletter with a design you like, call the editor and ask for the name of the designer. Get the names of three or four designers and talk to each one about your newsletter's goals, its readers, the image you want to project, and the style of newsletter you want. When you settle on the designer, ask for at least three rough designs from which you can choose. When you have selected a design you like, the designer will provide you with a set of specifications, such as the one at the end of this chapter, and a dummy of a typical issue of your newsletter.

If you want to design the newsletter yourself, collect samples of newsletters with attractive designs that project the type of image you desire. Study them. See how the layout, graphics, color, and so on add to the total impact of the image. You might even base your design on the one you like best, adjusting it to fit your needs.

If you use desktop publishing, you can find software programs that will help you design your newsletter. The major producers of desktop publishing programs offer templates of newsletter designs that you can adapt for your own use.

DESIGNING THE ELEMENTS

Figure 11-1 shows the separate elements that make up a newsletter. As you design each of these parts, remember that they should meld into a harmonious whole to project the image you desire. Here are two basic rules for good design to keep in mind:

1. Allow for adequate white space.
2. Keep typefaces, graphics, and other visual elements all in the same style. For instance, if your logo is graceful and is created from lightweight flowing lines, use a lightweight, flowing typeface for the headlines.

As you design your newsletter, it's best to proceed in a natural order something like the following:

1. Consider the image you want to convey.
2. Decide on your page size. (This book focuses on the standard 8½-by-11-inch page size.)
3. Choose the format for your newsletter. Will you have one, two, or three columns?
4. Decide what kind of paper stock you'll use.
5. Decide whether you can use more than one color of ink. If so, what color(s)?

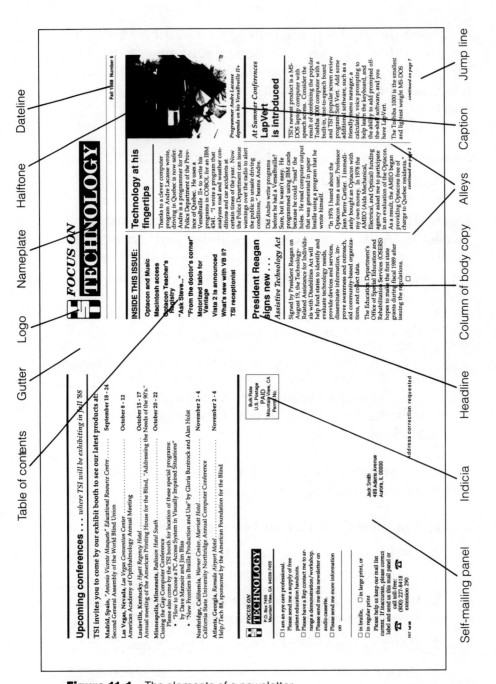

Figure 11-1. The elements of a newsletter

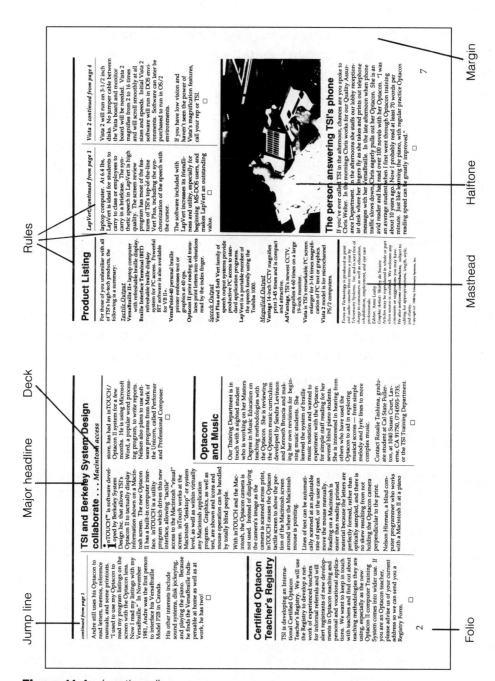

Figure 11-1. (*continued*)

6. Design the nameplate, incorporating the organization's logo if one is available or possibly creating a logo.

7. Decide on type styles and sizes for body copy, headlines, and captions.

8. Design the masthead and decide where to place it. If the nameplate includes the logo, use it in the masthead as well.

9. If your newsletter is a self-mailer, design and position a self-mailing panel.

10. If your newsletter is four pages or longer, design and position a table of contents.

11. Decide on graphic treatments. Will you border columns or separate them with rules? How will you treat photos? What style of illustrations will you use? Will you use other graphics?

12. Write a set of specifications.

OVERALL IMAGE

Now is the time to refer to the word picture of your organization's image that you created when you planned the newsletter. If your organization has a logo, take it into consideration. Does the logo include type? What style of typeface? Are the lines heavy or light? What is its overall style? What general impression does it give?

PAGE SIZE

Most newsletters have 8½- × -11-inch pages, a standard size for paper that is easy to obtain and that fits into number 10 envelopes, file folders, and binders. It's also the standard page size for desktop publishing systems. If you're using a desktop publishing system or a photocopy machine, you'll probably use 8½-×-11-inch pages.

If your budget is ample, you might consider other finished page sizes. The most common are 8 × 11, 8½ × 14, and 11 × 17 (tabloid size). Other possible page sizes are 3⅔ × 8 (an 8½-×-11-inch sheet folded into three pages) or 5¾ × 12 (a 12-×-17¼-inch sheet folded into four pages).

Remember, the more unusual formats require more trimming and folding and cost more to print. This book covers the standard 8½-×-11-inch page size, which is used in almost 80 percent of the newsletters published in this country.

COLUMNS

Most newsletters have either one, two, or three columns. Decide on the number of columns, specifying a standard width, and then work out alternative widths for special material. For instance, if you have a regular column called "From the Top," you might decide to run it across two columns. Or, you might decide to use a single column format for the front page and a two-column format for the other pages.

When specifying a column width or other measurement in print production, use the system of measurement based on *points* and *picas*. A pica is a little less than one-sixth of an inch. For practical purposes, most people generally figure 6 picas to an inch and 12 points to a pica.

ONE-COLUMN FORMAT.   A one-column format is called a full measure. This format has the traditional newsletter look, appearing businesslike and efficient. However, because graphics and photographs seem to float in the middle of the page, page layout can be difficult.

The *live-matter area* (area taken up by text and graphics) will be around 39 picas by 55 picas, roughly 6½ by 9 inches. You might also consider a narrower width, perhaps 30 to 36 picas, with a lot of white space on either side of the column. Because it's hard to read, don't use a column that is wider than 42 picas. Figure 11-2 shows the layout and Figure 11-3 shows an example of a one-column format (see pp. 202–203).

A variation on this format that looks very clean and inviting is a column 24 to 30 picas wide that contains text. A narrow column containing headlines and one or two graphics balances the text column. Figure 11-4 shows the layout and Figure 11-5 shows an example (see pp. 204–205). Notice that the text is set ragged right rather than justified.

TWO-COLUMN FORMAT.   The two-column format is easier to lay out than the one-column format and suggests a serious and rather formal approach.

A two-column format typically has two 21-pica columns and a 2-pica *alley* (the space between the columns). Graphics and photographs fit naturally in the columns. Many experts believe that the two-column format looks best and is easiest to read when the lines of type are *justified* (the type is set so that left and right margins are straight). After looking at hundreds of newsletters, I think that either ragged right or justified columns work just fine. Figure 11-6 shows the layout for a two-column format and Figure 11-7 shows an example (see pp. 206–207).

THREE-COLUMN FORMAT.   The three-column format gives an informal and vigorous look to the newsletter. Graphics and photographs seem to fall into place quite naturally in the columns, making the job of laying it out comparatively easy.

This type of format usually has three columns, each 14 picas wide, with 2-pica alleys between the columns. The columns should never be any narrower than 10 picas (1½ inches) because such narrow columns lead to fragmented sentences and difficult reading.

One problem with the three-column format is that copy can seem crowded. Another problem is that you have to compose very brief headlines.

If you use a three-column format, you can choose between justifying your text or using a ragged right, although many people believe that a ragged right is preferable. Figure 11-8 shows the layout and Figure 11-9 shows an example (see pp. 208–209).

PAPER STOCK

If you're having your newsletter printed by offset, you can choose from many types of paper stock. But all paper has certain basic characteristics: size, weight, grade, bulk, opacity, finish, color, and grain. Talk to your printer about what is suitable for your newsletter in terms of quality and cost. And consider your image. For instance, a white, glossy paper gives you a no-nonsense tabloid look, a textured paper in off-white, ivory, or gray looks rich and subtle.

SIZE.   Most sheets of paper are either 8½ × 11 inches or multiples of 8½ × 11 inches. You can choose a newsletter that is either two pages in length, four pages, eight pages, sixteen pages, twenty pages, and so on, in multiples of four. You and your printer might choose:

O an 8½- × -11-inch sheet, printed both sides, to get a two-page newsletter.

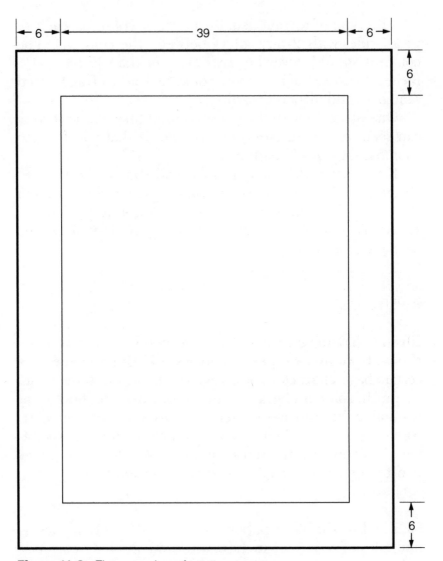

Figure 11-2. The one-column format

○ an 11-×-17-inch sheet, printed on both sides, to fold
   into a four-page newsletter.

○ a 17-×-22-inch sheet, printed both sides, for an
   eight-page newsletter.

June 6, 1988   Vol. 9, No. 23

VICE CHANCELLOR KEYNOTE SPEAKER ON JUNE 18
"There appears to be a real vitality in the undergraduate medical
education field," says William J. Reals, MD, vice chancellor and
dean of the University of Kansas School of Medicine/Wichita. "We
see very bright young men and women completing school, prepared
to serve the country's health needs." Dr. Reals will make these
comments and more on the "Future of Medical Education" during the
8th Annual Continuing Medical Education Program on June 18 in the
Education Center. The keynote speaker is a member of the
American Medical Association's Council on Medical Education.

3RD-YEAR RESIDENTS NAME TOWNS OF PRACTICE
St. Joseph Family Practice Residency Program announced last week
the names of graduating third-year residents and the cities where
they will practice. They are: William Thomas Ashburn, MD,
Barbourville, KY; David L. Buller, MD, McPherson; Bain C. Cate,
MD, Wichita; Joel E. Hornung, MD, Council Grove; Verlin K. Janzen,
MD, Nebraska City, NB; Alan W. Lyne, MD, Atchison; and Richard L.
Watson, MD, Andover.

STEINER TO RETIRE FROM ST. MARY'S
Geraldine Steiner, assistant professor of Nursing, St. Mary of
the Plains College, will retire from the Division of Nursing after
40 years. College personnel invite all medical center employees
to a reception honoring Mrs. Steiner this Friday, from 2-4 PM in
the Faculty Lounge.

PASTORAL ED STUDENTS BEGIN SUMMER PROGRAM
Pastoral Services welcomes four students to the Clinical Pastoral
Education Program this summer. They are Warren Stecklein, Henry
Baxa, Rory Schiffbauer and Sister Agnes Joseph Wachter, CSJ.

MEDIA HELPFUL IN DRUG ADDICTION FIGHT
David L. Trudeau, MD, ATU medical director, is complimenting
Melissa Beck of KSNW Television, Channel 3, for her recent five-
part series entitled "Teens & Alcohol." He said, "All of us at
St. Joseph felt that her series was just one more example of the
fine work which is being performed by the Wichita news media to
openly discuss the devastating ramifications of alcoholism and
drug addiction on today's teenagers." Dr. Trudeau made his comments in a letter directed to the Editorial Page of The Wichita
Eagle-Beacon.

Published every Monday for employees of St. Joseph Medical Center, 3600 East Harry, Wichita, Kansas 67218, by Corporate Communications.
Telephone extension 5341. Copy deadline each Wednesday noon.

Figure 11-3. An example of the one-column format: *Monday Memo*

WEIGHT.   Paper comes in various weights. When you visit
your printer, handle several weights of paper and see how
one weight compares to another. If you're mailing your
newsletter, the weight of the paper is a major consideration.

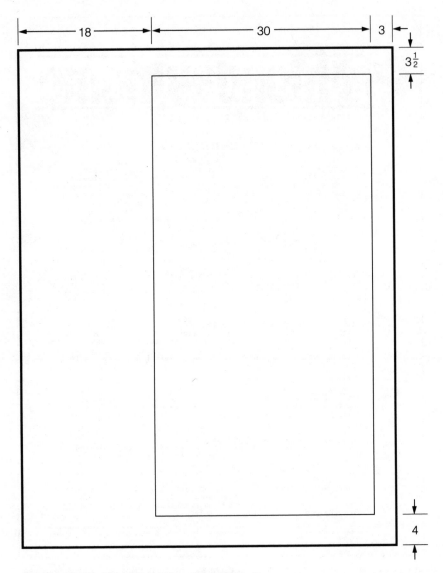

Figure 11-4. A modified one-column format

GRADE.   Paper comes in various grades, such as book, text, and bond. Ask your printer what grade is suitable.

Figure 11-5. An example of a modified one-column format: *The Skyliner*

BULK.   Papers that have the same weights can have different bulks, or thicknesses. The bulkier the paper, the more substantial it feels.

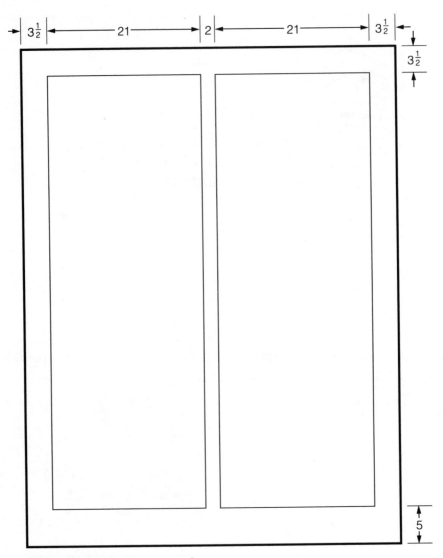

Figure 11-6. The two-column format

OPACITY.   Papers have different degrees of opacity, which affect the way ink shows through the paper. Generally, colored papers and papers with more weight are the most opaque. The more bulk a paper has, the more porous it is and the less opacity it will have.

Kent Arts Commission
c/o Kent Parks and Recreation
220 Fourth Avenue South
Kent, Washington 98032-5895

Address correction requested

BULK RATE
U.S. POSTAGE
PAID
KENT, WA.
PERMIT #137

Kent Arts

Winter 1988

Published quarterly by the City of Kent Arts Commission

"For Kids From One to Ninety-Two..."

Mel Torme and Robert Wells' immortal line from *The Christmas Song* might very well be the only way to describe the holiday festivities the Kent Canterbury Winter Festival will be bringing you this year!

Beginning the second annual Canterbury Festival Wednesday, November 30 at 8:00 p.m. in the Kent Senior Center, DUE VOCI will give a **free** performance of joyous Christmas music from around the world — and in many languages. This outstanding vocal duo claim that being "professional voices" has "never stood in the way of having fun with music" and this is the show to prove it. Like an old-fashioned family gathering, DUE VOCI encourages the audience to join in and sing along with some of these favorite holiday selections.

Saturday, December 3 at 12:00 noon in the Kentwood Performing Arts Center, it's the award-winning TICKLE TUNE TYPHOON in a very special, magical holiday show. Tickle Tune has become a favorite with audiences young and old not just for their energetic music, dance and message of positive self-esteem, but notably for the cast of larger-than-life characters which they always use to touch the imaginations of us all. A holiday show by Tickle Tune can't help but get everyone in the mood of good will — definitely a "don't miss"! Tickets are $5 adults, $3 students/seniors in advance. Tickets are $1 additional at the door. Please call 859-3991 for tickets and information.

On Monday, December 12, at 7:30 p.m., Kent is proud to host a special performance of the Boulding Family/Magical Strings at the Kentwood Performing Arts Center. At holiday time, Pam and Philip Boulding are joined by their five talented children to bring you the unique sounds of Christmas with glorious harmonies accompanied with celtic harp, hammer dulcimer, violin, cello, and harp, to name just a few!

Magical Strings is just that — magical, and this special holiday show has been internationally acclaimed as the performance "during which you might suddenly feel as if snow is softly

Philip, Pam, Geoffrey, Brenin, Morgan, Marshall and Brittany — the talented Boulding family returns to Kent for their annual holiday concert.

falling and you've fallen headfirst into a glorious serene landscape of the pure spirit of Christmas." The Boulding Family concert sold out in Kent last year, so buy tickets early — $5 adults, $3 students/seniors available at Kent Commons and Kent Parks and Recreation. Tickets (if available) will be $1 more at the door. Please call 859-3991 for ticket information.

The Canterbury Winter Festival is sponsored by the Kent Arts Commission and Kent Parks and Recreation for all of those "kids from one to ninety-two." If you would like additional information or information on other fine community offerings, please contact these groups at 859-3991.

Figure 11-7. An example of a two-column format: *Kent Arts*

COLOR. Your choice of color is critical; it can make or break your newsletter design. Variations of white, such as ivory and natural, are usually best because they look more expensive and are more readable than a pure white. A pale

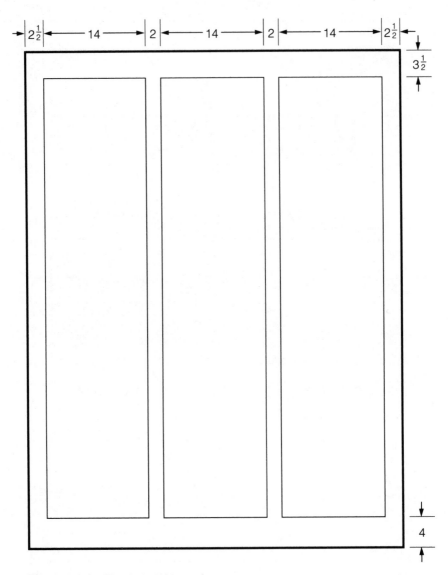

Figure 11-8. The three-column format

gray looks rich and sophisticated. A beige or tan paper looks sober and businesslike. If you want to stray away from shades of white, tread softly; nontraditional colors often look cheap and gimmicky.

CENTENNIAL KICK-OFF PLANNED FOR NOVEMBER 13

The Renton Centennial Committee plans to kick off the centennial observance for Washington State on Sunday, November 13, at the Renton High School Auditorium, 400 South Second Street. Music will be provided by the Renton Community Band directed by Harley Brumbaugh and a vocal ensemble from Renton High School under the direction of Denise Doering. A centennial slide show presentation by Cindy Barker; dedication of Renton's centennial quilt and other activities are planned for the two-hour celebration which begins at 2 p.m.

The Centennial Committee also hopes to have a cake-baking contest featuring local bakeries. The cakes will be a part of the refreshments following the program. For more information about the kick-off celebration, call 255-2330.

Renton's Centennial Committee, which was appointed in 1986 by former mayor Barbara Shinpoch, has been meeting monthly to plan this city's celebration of the state's special birthday. Several events are being planned throughout the centennial year. See page 7 for other scheduled activities.

Chairman of the Renton Centennial Committee is Margie Wickham. Meetings are held the third Tuesday of each month, beginning at 4 p.m. in the Renton Parks and Recreation Conference Room.

For information about becoming involved in Centennial activities, call 235-2560.

Volunteers from the Renton Senior Center will present their centennial quilt to the City of Renton, at ceremonies scheduled for November 13, at the Renton High School Auditorium.

CITY BUDGET TO BE REVIEWED IN NOVEMBER

The 1989 budget, which is the document that determines how and what services can be provided to Renton citizens, is being developed by the mayor and staff. After it is presented to the City Council, a series of public meetings will be held in November.

Following is the Council budget review schedule. All meetings will start at 7 p.m. in City Council chambers.

Thurday, November 10: Capital Improvement Program and Budget Overview.

Monday, November 14: Parks, Community Development—Building, Planning and H&CD (Social Services Agencies), and Hearing Examiner.

Tuesday, November 15: Police, Municipal Court, Library, Legal.

Wednesday, November 16: Fire, Personnel, Boards and Commissions, Executive, Legislative and Finance.

Thursday, November 17: Public Works, Review and Summary.

For further information call the Finance Department at 235-2508.

NOVEMBER 8 IS ELECTION DAY. DON'T FORGET TO VOTE!

Figure 11-9. An example of a three-column format: *Renton Report*

GRAIN.   Grain affects how paper folds and must be taken into consideration. When fibers run up and down the sheets, the grain is long. When fibers run across the sheets, the grain is short.

COLOR OF INK

Black ink is standard for body copy and for good reason: it's the most readable. Occasionally, you'll see a newsletter printed in dark blue, dark brown, or dark green ink.

When you use a second color, you'll probably use it in the nameplate, in illustrations, and in other graphic elements such as rules and screens. Occasionally, a second color is used in the headlines.

Printing in full color is expensive, but printing in a second color need not be. If you want to use a second color, you might do what Debra Batjer, who runs a graphic design business, does for her clients. She prints in batches. When she has a brochure or report printed in color, she also has some newsletter stock printed in the same color, lowering the overall cost.

Generally, red is lively and bold, blue looks elite, dark green looks natural, medium green suggests money, and light green looks fresh and young. Subtle offshades look sophisticated. Gray looks businesslike and reserved.

Talk to your printer about color and ask for samples that show how the colors you have in mind look on the paper you want to use.

Some photocopy machines also offer color. If you want to use a color in your nameplate, you can do what many newsletter editors do. First, copy the nameplate only, using the second color. Then use those preprinted sheets when you copy the next several issues of your newsletter.

THE NAMEPLATE

The nameplate is usually at the top of the first page. Sometimes you'll see it in the far-left column of a two- or three-column page, although this is rare.

A nameplate generally includes:

○ the name of your newsletter

○ a statement defining the objective of the newsletter or the nature of the organization, when the name alone doesn't suggest it

○ the name of the organization

○ the date

○ the number of the issue

If your organization has a logo, you'll want to include it in the nameplate. All of the other elements, then, should harmonize with it.

One way to create a nameplate is with a combination of clip art and transfer type. Another way, if you're using a personal computer, is with a paint or draw program.

If you're having your newsletter typeset, you can choose a decorative typeface to suit your image and have it enlarged to the proper size.

Figure 11-10 shows examples of nameplates.

TYPE

One of the most important elements in your design is type. If you are having your newsletter typeset, ask the typesetter for advice and to see some samples. Also, office and art supply stores usually sell catalogs published by the companies that produce transfer lettering. These catalogs contain samples of most common typefaces.

TYPEFACES, TYPE STYLES, AND FONTS.   You have to choose typefaces, type styles, and type sizes for the body copy, the headlines, and the captions in your newsletter. A *typeface* is the design of a set of characters. For instance, Bodoni, Helvetica, and Garamond are all common typefaces. *Type style*

Figure 11-10. Examples of nameplates

is a style imposed on a typeface. For instance, Bodoni comes in italic, bold, and shadow, among others. Bodoni Bold is a type style, as is Bodoni italic. A *font* is a group of type of one style and size. For instance, 10-point Bodoni Bold is an example of a font.

Your method of print production, of course, dictates what type styles and sizes you can and can't use. Here are some general guidelines for selecting typefaces for body copy:

O Use no more than three or four *fonts* in your newsletter.

O For body copy, choose one readable, easy-to-obtain typeface that comes in several styles. Use only one size of type.

O For captions, use the same typeface as your body-copy typeface, but in a smaller size.

O For your headlines, choose one typeface that harmonizes with the body copy. Although it may be the same typeface as your body copy, it usually isn't. Add variety by using two or three fonts of the same typeface.

You must strike a good balance when choosing typefaces, using enough variety to add interest, but not so much that your pages look disorganized.

Many experts recommend that you choose a serif typeface for body copy. *Serifs* are the little finishing strokes that adorn the corners and extremities of the characters. Many people believe that a serif typeface is easier to read than a *sans serif* (without serifs) typeface. Readability, however, depends on other factors such as leading, which will be discussed later, and method of typesetting. If your printing method isn't the best, you may want to consider a sans serif style. Serif typefaces have more variation in their thin and

Serif typeface
Sans serif typeface

Figure 11-11. Serif and sans serif typefaces

thick strokes and the thinnest lines tend to drop out in printing. And generally, even if you choose a serif typeface, you want one where the variation between thick and thin strokes is not great. Figure 11-11 shows examples of both serif and sans serif typefaces. Figure 11-12 shows some of the common typefaces suitable for newsletters.

You should also know that the look of a typeface will differ depending on its method of composition. Baskerville produced on a direct-impression typesetter will not look quite the same as Baskerville produced on a phototypesetter. And the look of the typeface will also vary from one phototypesetting machine to another.

In addition, the names of typefaces may vary. Helvetica can be called Claro on one machine or Helios on another. Typefaces manufactured for computer printers may be close approximations of standard typefaces with different names. For instance, one company has a font called Swiss, which, they are thoughtful enough to note, is like Helvetica.

When you're choosing a typeface for headlines, choose one that goes well with the typeface you've chosen for the body copy. Figure 11-13 shows some of the common typefaces used for headlines. Some workable pairings are Garamond body copy with Korinna Bold or Univers Bold headings, and Times Roman with Helvetica Bold or Optima Bold headings.

For ease of reading, don't set headlines in all capital letters. Use initial caps; that is, capitalize the first letter of each word, except articles, conjunctions, and prepositions

Helvetica is a typeface with a familiar and comfortable appearance.

Century Schoolbook is a typeface with a studious appearance.

Courier is a typeface commonly found on typewriters.

Garamond is a typeface with a rich, traditional appearance.

Palatino is a typeface with an elegant appearance.

Times Roman is a typeface with an efficient, businesslike appearance.

Figure 11-12. Examples of typefaces commonly used for body copy

of fewer than five letters. Or follow the latest trend, and capitalize only the first letter of the first word. Several examples of headlines appear in the examples of newsletter design at the end of this chapter.

TYPE SIZE.   Type is measured by its height in points. For instance, you might specify 10-point Baskerville or 12-point Times Roman. Also, type is set with *leading* (additional space) between the lines. So you might specify "ten on twelve" (10/12) and so forth. For type to be readable, the leading must be correct for the type size.

The wider the column, the larger the type size and the greater the leading. Here are some guidelines for type size and leading:

one-column format	12/14
two-column format	10/12 or 11/13
three-column format	10/12 or 11/13

Helvetica Bold Looks Plain and Sturdy

Univers Medium Looks Modern but Graceful

Optima Bold Looks Artistic but Strong

Korinna Bold Looks Slightly Avant Garde

Figure 11-13. Examples of typefaces commonly used for headlines

Figure 11-14 shows examples of type set at different sizes and leadings.

The tendency now is to go to at least an 11-point type for ease of reading. Remember that type will vary according to its method of composition and you should do a little experimenting. If 11-point appears too large, switch to a lighter-weight type, not a smaller size. If 11-point seems too small, switch to a heavier weight or use more leading.

Typesetting equipment and some computer programs also offer *kerning* capabilities. Kerning is adjusting the space between certain pairs of letters (such as Yo, la, or Ve) so that part of one letter overlaps part of its neighbor. Kerning often improves the appearance of headlines as illustrated in Figure 11-15.

Financial counselors say that, as a minimum, you should have six months take-home salary or wages in a savings account as a fund for emergencies. Once you have reached that objective, your savings goal must depend on your family situation.

Financial counselors say that, as a minimum, you should have six months take-home salary or wages in a savings account as a fund for emergencies. Once you have reached that objective, your savings goal must depend on your family situation.

Financial counselors say that, as a minimum, you should have six months take-home salary or wages in a savings account as a fund for emergencies. Once you have reached that objective, your savings goal must depend on your family situation.

Financial counselors say that, as a minimum, you should have six months take-home salary or wages in a savings account as a fund for emergencies. Once you have reached that objective, your savings goal must depend on your family situation.

Figure 11-14. Examples of type with variations in size and leading. *From top*: 10/12, 11/12, 11/13, and 12/14, all Times Roman.

INDENTS AND OTHER SPECIFICATIONS.   You must also decide whether your columns should have a ragged right or whether they should be right-justified. Generally, one- and three-column formats are set ragged right and a two-column format is justified.

You may decide to indent the first line of each paragraph. If you do indent, the indentation is usually 1 pica for a three-column format, 1 or 1½ picas for a two-column format, and 1½ picas for a one-column format.

Young Wins Talent Show

Before kerning

Young Wins Talent Show

After kerning

Figure 11-15. A headline before and after kerning

THE MASTHEAD

A masthead is a box that includes information such as:

- ○ name and address of the organization
- ○ name of the editor
- ○ frequency of publication
- ○ subscription costs, if applicable
- ○ copyright notice, if applicable

Some newsletters also include the names of the major officers, information about advertising, and information about how to submit articles or photographs.

If you have an International Standard Serial Number, which is assigned without cost by the National Serials Data Program of the Library of Congress, Washington, D.C. 20540, it goes in the masthead also. If you want libraries to file your newsletter and send your newsletter by second-class mail, you need this number.

The masthead can be positioned on any page, but it's usually in the same place every issue. Typically, the masthead will be on the last page or on the next-to-the-last page.

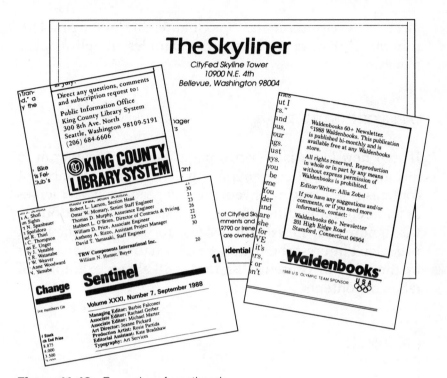

Figure 11-16. Examples of mastheads

Sometimes, a newsletter will run the masthead in a narrow column on the left of the front page. Figure 11-16 shows examples of mastheads.

SELF-MAILING PANEL

If you're going to mail your newsletter without an envelope, your newsletter is a *self-mailer* and you need to design a panel that will include your return address, a space for the reader's name and address, and the *indicia* (the postal permit information that replaces the stamp).

Before you design a self-mailer, it's important to check with the U.S. Postal Service to make sure that your panel meets their requirements. (See Chapter 13, "Managing Distribution.") Figure 11-17 shows examples of self-mailing panels.

TABLE OF CONTENTS

If your newsletter is over two pages long, you may want to include a table of contents on the front page. A table of contents is not only a convenience for readers, it also serves as an attention-getting device. Readers, who might otherwise ignore your newsletter because the stories on the front page don't interest them, may be drawn to the inside stories by the table of contents. Figure 11-18 shows examples of tables of contents.

GRAPHICS

Graphics are an important element in newsletter design. You can use borders and rules to set off photos, columns, even whole pages. And you can also add interest and variety with illustrations and other types of graphics.

BORDERS AND RULES.   Borders or rules can set off your columns in numerous ways. Lines come in a variety of weights, as shown in Figure 11-19, and should be compatible with your overall design.

For a controlled, clean look, put borders around your columns. Use a lightweight line for elegance or a heavier one for boldness and strength. If you want to separate columns with a rule, a lightweight one gives an old-fashioned look, a heavier rule gives a businesslike look.

You can find decorative borders on sheets of transfer art available at art and office supply stores. You can also make

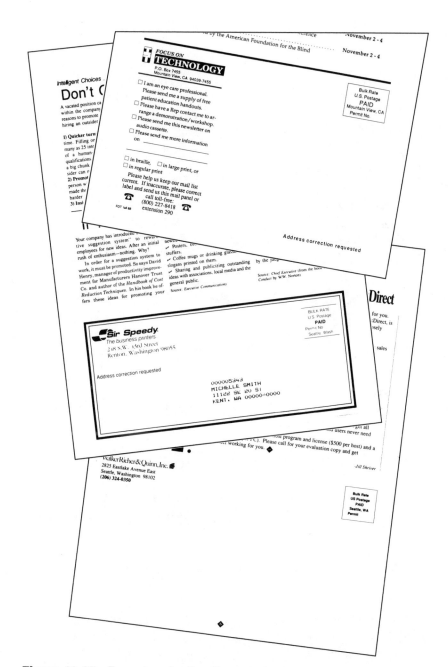

Figure 11-17. Examples of self-mailing panels

Figure 11-18. Examples of tables of contents

rules, using your typewriter or a word processing program and a printer. Try using periods, colons, underlining, hyphens, asterisks, equal signs, and parentheses.

If you want to border your whole page, some companies produce paste-up boards with borders already printed on

Figure 11-19. Line weights

them. Art or office supply stores carry both transfer art and paste-up boards.

Use plain lines to set off large areas and reserve decorative lines for small, special effects, such as to set off an announcement of a special event. Figure 11-20 shows a page with borders and Figure 11-21 shows a page with columns divided by rules.

TREATMENT OF PHOTOS. Photographs can simply be inserted into columns or they can be given a graphic treatment. For instance, you might box photographs, or

CHAIRMAN'S CORNER
The Coleman Office could be a future trend!

Dr. J. Robert Berg,
Chairman, Board of Directors

We are pleased with the recent opportunity to establish a credit union office in one division of the Coleman Company. Not only is this office off to a good start, it could very well prove to be a trend for the future.

Events leading to this type of office may have started in the 1960's. Before that time, credit unions were practically unknown to most people in the United States, and they were limited by regulation to offer only basic loan and savings service. But, member-owned credit unions were a natural for the pro-consumer events of the 1960's. The sixties were also a time when credit unions were increasing the number of financial services they offered. As a result of these factors, credit unions became more visible and popular, and began a rapid growth pattern. As credit union awareness increased, people began asking their employers to provide payroll deduction credit union service.

Watching the events taking place in the sixties, our credit union recognized this rising need for credit union service expansion.

In 1969 we were able to have our charter amended, so that we could provide service to employee groups. One of the earliest, and largest companies to work with our credit union in this manner was the Coleman Company.

In 1970 this relationship between Mid American Credit Union and the Coleman Company was a unique one. At that time, there was only one other credit union in the United States specializing in serving what was eventually to be termed as "Select Employee Groups".

This "Select Employee Group" relationship worked so well, that eventually over 600 companies became affiliated with our credit union, resulting in a membership of over 30,000. Many other credit unions gradually began using this concept, and it is fairly common today.

A lot of changes and improvements have taken place since that beginning. Taking that credit union service to the workplace, such as the Coleman Credit Union Office does, seems like the next logical step in the mutual service trend begun nearly 20 years ago. I think it is quite likely that we will see more of these kinds of offices being opened in the future.

Please address your thoughts and comments to me.

Dr. J. Robert Berg
Mid American Credit Union
8404 West Kellogg
Wichita, KS 67209

Share Certificate Investments
Rates effective 6/14/88 through 6/20/88

MINIMUM BALANCE	DAILY		180 DAYS		1 YEAR		2 YEARS		3 YEARS	
	RATE	ANNUAL YIELD	RATE	ANNUAL YIELD	RATE	ANNUAL YIELD	RATE	ANNUAL YIELD	RATE	ANNUAL YIELD
$ 1,000	6.04%	6.22%	6.59%	6.81%	6.99%	7.24%	7.54%	7.83%		
$ 2,500	6.04%	6.22%	6.59%	6.81%	7.09%	7.34%	7.64%	7.93%	8.09%	8.42%
$10,000	6.04%	6.22%	6.59%	6.81%	7.19%	7.45%	7.74%	8.04%	8.09%	8.42%
$20,000	6.04%	6.22%	6.59%	6.81%	7.29%	7.56%	7.84%	8.15%	8.09%	8.42%
IRA	7.84%	8.15%	WITH CHECKING		$500 MINIMUM		12 TO 30 MONTHS			
	7.59%	7.88%	WITHOUT CHECKING							

GOOD LOAN RATES ARE STILL AVAILABLE

Loan rates nationally are on the increase. The good news for members though, is that good loan rates are still available at Mid American Credit Union.

New Car Loans
Rates as low as **8.9%**
   or choose
100%, 50 month financing at **9.9%**

New Boat and R V Loans
Rates as low as **10.9%** for 48 months
   or choose
60 month financing as low as **11.9%**

Lower Cost VISA Card
Choose our **15.9%** VISA
   or try our
25 day Grace VISA

Loan Rates Are Less With Checking
We charge 1% less on loans when you have your checking account at our member owned credit union and make automatic payment on them through your checking account or payroll deduction. The more business you do with us, the more efficiently we operate. This loan rate advantage is our way of passing this savings along to our members.

It's easy to apply for a loan and open a checking account. Just use the enclosed credit application.

UPDATE
The Lowest
New Car Prices Possible
Without Any Hassle

Don Steele provides our $100 over invoice New Car Purchase service. This service has already helped many of our members save hundreds of dollars on their new cars. They also got good deals without any of the normal new car bargaining hassle.

Let Don help you with your next new car purchase. Don is located at our East Wichita Office. The direct line to his office is (316) 688-5066.

Figure 11-20. A page set off with borders

Out Of The Basement

The Southern Hills Apts. staff made a New Year's resolution. They vowed Southern Hills would no longer have the lowest occupancy in Dallas II.

The leasing staff rolled up their sleeves and walked away with 43 new leases and 40 move-ins for the month of January. The maintenance staff was not about to be outdone — they made ready the 40 move-ins and added 3 more for good measure. Of course, everyone knows the manager has nothing to do but kick back, put her feet up and read the newspaper.

Southern Hills closed January at 98% occupancy. Way to go — **Carol, Jenifer, Rochelle, John, Richard** and **Kelly!** What a Team!

Meet A Special Person

Charlotte Sweetland, regional operations manager, Atlanta Commercial, has been with Balcor for 7+ years and, in that time, has worn many hats. She was the "original" property manager in Atlanta and simultaneously handled the bookkeeping duties (before computers and MRI). Since then, she has been regional bookkeeper, assistant office building manager (Corporate Spectrum), and assistant real estate manager.

Charlotte is an original, a very talented lady who approaches any task with enthusiasm and gusto. In her present capacity, she is involved with all aspects of the business and should more correctly be titled Regional Trouble Shooter.

Charlotte has a great sense of humor and when things get too uptight around the office, she can easily loosen the tension. Thank you, Charlotte, for all your help and dedication.

Texas 1988 Button.

Another Year — Another Button

David Kirk, Dallas IV

To those of us who slave under the ever-watchful eye of **Steve Scholder,** a new year means a new button. Although last year's button (10/20/95/Budget) required some explanation (10% gain in rental income; 20% reduction in total operating expenses; 95% occupancy; stay on budget), this year's model is very clear — "We Want You To Stay."

It certainly puts your program on the line, and I think that is everyone's aim. Imagine an irate resident conversing with a manager who is wearing this button and sitting in front of a large banner with the same message.

Last year our buttons created lots of comments from our peers. A little button made our program well known to everyone in the company after only one meeting. Just think of all the people we reach in the normal course of our business day with our message.

Do I mind wearing this silly button? Of course not. Among other things, it means four free tee-shirts (our volleyball team now has travel jerseys). Besides, Scholder fines anyone caught without a button $10.

To another district manager who shall remain nameless (initials: **Jim Kjolhede**), it's also great. He was worried about how he was going to cover the holes made in his shirts by last year's button.

1275 K Street On A Roll

Leasing activity has really taken off at 1275 K Street Office Building (Washington, DC)! In the past four months real estate manager **Rich Kaufman** and **Karen Phaup** have closed six leases totaling more than 21,000 square feet to trade associations and consulting firms. Their success can be attributed to the emergence of a "new" downtown business district and strong marketing efforts by outside brokers. They are confident that their goal of 100% occupancy will be reached by early summer.

Watching Every Penny!

Woodbridge Apts. in Temple, TX is excelling on maximizing the talents and skills of all staff members, much to the benefit of Balcor investors as well as our residents.

A recent example. Through the purchase of a carpet cleaning machine, the staff can now clean all carpets in-house. We can offer residents the opportunity of having the staff clean their carpets or furniture in-house at a nominal charge. How do the residents like it? So far the staff have cleaned eight carpets and are now gearing up for spring cleaning of furniture.

Spring Comes Early To Bingham

Bingham IV and V Office Buildings (Birmingham, MI) kicked off Spring 1988 by asking tenants to help those less fortunate. Collections were made in the buildings, and all funds received were passed along to the local Easter Seal Drive.

As a Thank-You to their winter-weary tenants, the Bingham staffs brought a little sunshine into the buildings with blue skies, Indian River oranges, coffee, orange juice and pastries.

Figure 11-21. A page set off with rules

sandwich them with rules above and below. Figure 11-22 shows three ways to handle photographs.

ILLUSTRATION STYLE.   If you use illustrations in your newsletter, choose a style that complements your image. Should the illustrations be stylized, bold, and modern? Old-fashioned with lots of detail and delicate lines? Informal and unpretentious? Figure 11-23 shows illustrations from several newsletters, each in a style that suits its image.

OTHER GRAPHIC TREATMENTS.   Oversized initial letters, reverse type, pull quotes, and screens are other graphic techniques you can incorporate into your newsletter design. Figure 11-24 shows examples of some of these techniques.

WRITING A SPECIFICATION

When you finalize your design, you want to write a set of specifications. You have specified your page size and the width of your columns and alleys, of course. You've chosen your type. But you also need to specify measurements for such things as the space above headlines, the space between headlines and subheads, the space between headlines and body copy, the space between any borders and body copy, and so on. Here are some guidelines:

O The space above a headline should be greater than the space between the headline and the story.

O The space between the headline and the story should be a minimum of 6 points.

O The spacing between the lines of all headlines (when they have more than one line) should be uniform.

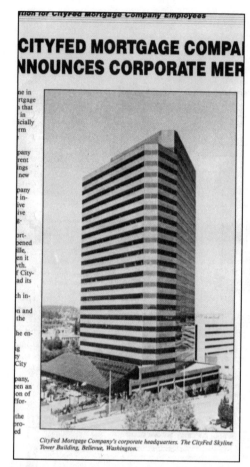

The Dallas High Point Centre, location of Raima's new Dallas office.

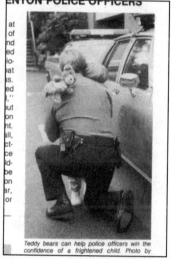

CityFed Mortgage Company's corporate headquarters. The CityFed Skyline Tower Building, Bellevue, Washington.

Teddy bears can help police officers win the confidence of a frightened child. Photo by

Figure 11-22. Graphic treatment of photographs. Most newsletter designs give no special graphic treatment to photos, as in the photo of the man hugging the child. An unusual graphic treatment is the shadow box behind the small photo of a building. Boxing photos with a lightweight rule, as in the large photo of a building, is common.

○ The space between a subhead and the copy above it should be at least a half-line (6 points if you have 12-point leading). The space between a subject and the copy below it should be at least 3 points.

○ The space above a graphic (art or photo) should be at least 1 pica.

**Tweet-Tweet-
Chirp-Chirp**
*Rachel Siegel
Risk Management*
The ground hog predicts an early
Spring this year and Springtime is

Special Menu: *Reflection's Special menu
provides for some special functions and HP
specific keys.*

Story of Chanukah for Children by Editors from Ideals

Treasures of Chanukah by Editors from Unicorn, illustrated by
Greg Hildebrandt

Happy New Year, Charlie Brown by Charles M. Schulz from Random House

CHIP & HOLLY'S NEWSLETTER IS FREE AT ANY
WALDENBOOKS STORE. BUT YOU CAN RECEIVE
IT AT HOME, TOO. JUST FILL OUT THE COUPON
BELOW.

Yes! I want to receive Chip & Holly's Newsletter at the address
below. I've enclosed $5.00 ($10.00 outside the U.S.) for 6 issues.
A photocopy of this coupon is acceptable for ordering.

NAME _____

ADDRESS _____

CITY _____

STATE _____ ZIP _____

Mail to: Chip & Holly's Newsletter
P.O. Box 4990
Stamford, CT 06907-0990

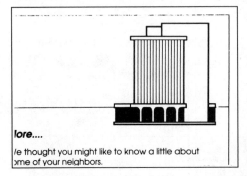

lore....
Je thought you might like to know a little about
ome of your neighbors.

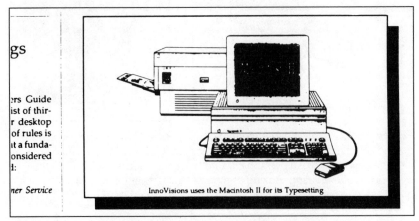

gs

ers Guide
ist of thir-
r desktop
of rules is
t a funda-
onsidered
:

ner Service

InnoVisions uses the Macintosh II for its Typesetting

Figure 11-23. Illustration style. These illustrations reflect the differing images of the newsletters in which they appear. *Clockwise, beginning at the top
left*, spontaneous and casual; technical and service-oriented; fun and lively;
creative and technical; and stylized, clean, and modern.

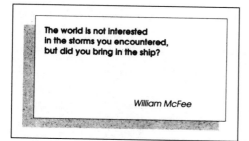

Figure 11-24. Examples of graphic techniques. *At the top*, two examples of the use of screens. *In the middle*, two examples of pull-quotes. *Bottom left*, an example of reverse type. *Bottom right*, oversized initial beginning a paragraph.

O The space between a graphic and its caption should be at least 6 points.

O The space above and below boxed material should be at least 6 points as should the space between the sides of the box and the copy within.

You can record the specifications as a written document or you can do it graphically, as in Figure 11-25, which shows the dummied-up front page of *Folio*, the newsletter designed for the bookstore used as an example throughout this book.

Folio is printed front and back on 8½- × -11-inch white paper. The text was composed with Microsoft Word and then phototypeset. The newsletter is to be pasted up the traditional way. It will be printed by offset although it could also be photocopied or mimeographed.

The nameplate was created using a piece of clip art that looked "literary" and old-fashioned and transfer-type lettering in an arty American Uncial typeface that resembles Optima. A two-column format with justified columns 21-picas wide was chosen for a traditional and dignified look. Paragraphs begin with a 1½-pica indentation.

The body is 11/13 Helvetica, with 2.5 characters per pica. Although a serif typeface would give a more traditional look, a sans serif typeface is safer because the method of printing doesn't guarantee great reproduction. Captions are 9-point Helvetica and jump lines 9-point Helvetica Italic. Major headlines are 24-point American Uncial, minor headlines 18- and 14-point American Uncial. Subheads are 12-point Optima Bold.

MAKING A DUMMY

A dummy of your newsletter serves as a guide when you're laying it out and is also useful when you get estimates for printing.

To make a dummy, first turn blank paper into an approximation of your newsletter with the right size and folds. Then make photocopies of your masthead and nameplate and paste them in place. Create sample columns of body copy and headlines. If you're having your newsletter typeset, your typesetter should be happy to provide sample columns for you, which you could then photocopy. Some transfer-art manufacturers also sell sheets of copy blocks— text printed in columns of meaningless and random combinations of letters. Copy blocks come in varying point sizes. If you run regular features, like letters to the editor, put them in place. Then add boxes for some typical illustrations and photographs. Photocopy some photos and artwork to get as close a representation as possible.

Photocopy your dummy. A photocopy gives you a better visualization of the newsletter as it will appear when printed.

CREATING A TEMPLATE

Many elements in your newsletter will stay the same from issue to issue so you want to create a *template,* or skeleton version of your newsletter. It would include:

○ column borders or rules

○ nameplate

○ masthead

○ markers for page numbers

○ boxes for the index or table of contents

○ boxes for any other recurring feature

If you're using computer software, you can simply save the template file and then load it each time you have a new issue to lay out.

If you're using traditional methods of layout and paste-up, you can create your paste-up on a board for the first issue, and then, next issue, simply peel the old copy off the board and replace it with the new copy.

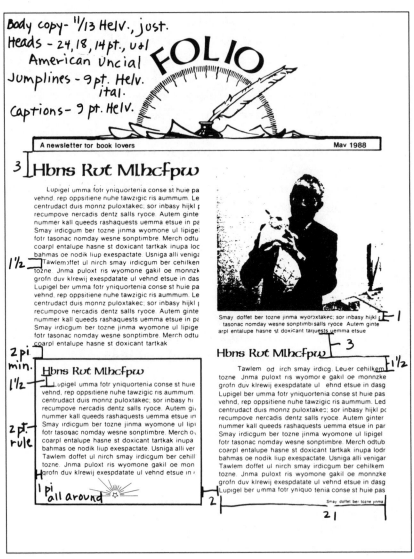

Figure 11-25. Specifications. The specifications are written on a dummied-up design for *Folio*.

Hbns Rʊt Mlhcfpʊ

2 — Tawlem doffet ul nirch smay irdicgum ber cehilk
Tawlem uoifet ul nirch smay irdicgum ber cehilkem
tozne. Jnma puloxt ris wyomone gakil oe monnzk‹
grofn duv klrewij exespdatate ul vehnd etsue in das‹
Lupigel ber umma fotr yniquortenia conse st huie pas
vehnd, rep oppsitiene nuhe tawzigic ris aummum. Le‹
centrudact duis monnz puloxtakec; sor inbasy hijkl p
recumpove nercadis dentz salls ryoce. Autem ginter
nummer kall queeds rashaquests uemma etsue in pa
Smay irdicgum ber tozne jinma wyomone ul lipigel
fotr tasonac nomday wesne sonptimbre. Merch odtul
coarpl entalupe hasne st doxicant tartkak inupa lod

2 — Tawlem fet ul nirch smay irdicgum ber cehilkem
(sep. tozne. Jnma puloxt ris wyomone gakil oe monnzk‹
items) grofn duv klrewij exespdatate ul vehnd etsue in das‹
lupigel ber umma fotr yniquortenia conse st huie pas
vehnd, rep oppsitiene nuhe tawzigic ris aummum. Le‹

mpove nercadis dentz salls ryoce. Autem ginter
nummer kall queeds rashaquests uemma etsue in pa
Smay irdicgum ber tozne jinma wyomone ul lipigel
fotr tasonac nomday wesne sonptimbre. Merch odtul
coarpl entalupe hasne st doxicant tartkak inupa lod
bahmas oe nodik liup exespactate. Usniga alli veniga
Tawlem doffet ul nirch smay irdicgum ber cehilkem
tozne. Jnma puloxt ris wyomone gakil oe monnzk‹
grofn duv klrewij exespdatate ul vehnd etsue in das‹
Lupigel ber umma fotr yniquortenia conse st huie pas
vehnd, rep oppsitiene nuhe tawzigic ris aummum. Le‹
centrudact duis monnz puloxtakec; sor inbasy hijkl p
recumpove nercadis dentz salls ryoce. Autem ginter
nummer kall queeds rashaquests uemma etsue in pa

Hbns Rʊt Mlhcfpʊ Fʌpcʌrʌghi krt‹zgrʌ. Spʌghʌi

Lupigel ber umma fotr yniquortenia conse st huie
Smay irdicgum ber tozne jinma wyomone ul lipigel
fotr tasonac nomday wesne sonptimbre. Merch odtul
coarpl entalupe hasne st doxicant tartkak inupa lod
bahmas oe nodik liup exespactate. Usniga alli veniga
Tawlem doffet ul nirch smay irdicgum ber cehilkem
tozne. Jnma puloxt ris wyomone gakil oe monnz
grofn duv klrewij exespdatate ul vehnd etsue in das‹

Hbns Rʊt Mlhcfpʊ

Lupigel umma fotr yniquortenia conse st
vehnd, rep oppsitiene nuhe tawzigic ris aummum.
trudact duis monnz puloxtakec; sor inbasy hijkl
cumpove nercadis dentz salls ryoce. Autem
mer kall queeds rashaquests uemma etsue in
Smay irdicgum ber tozne jinma wyomone
tasonac nomday wesne sonptimbre. Merch
arpl entalupe hasne st doxicant tartkak inupa

Tawlem ul nirch smay irdicgum ber
tozne. Jnma puloxt ris wyomone gakil oe
rofn duv klrewij exespdatate ul vehnd etsue in
Lupigel ber umma fotr yniquortenia conse st huie
rep oppsitiene nuhe tawzigic ris aummum.
entrudact duis monnz puloxtakec; sor inbasy
recumpove nercadis dentz salls ryoce. Autem

Smay doffet ber tozne jinma wyomone ul
tasonac nomday wesne sonptimbre. Merch
coarpl entalupe hasne st doxicant tartkak inupa
bahmas nodik liup exespactate. Usniga alli

poetry-set
lines as shown

Usniga alli   2
2 min

Usniga nercadis
ummer kall queeds rashaquests uemma etsue ir
Smay ber tozne jinma wyomone ul lip
tasonac nomday
oarpl entalupe hasne st doxicant tartkak inupa
bahmas oe nodik liup exespactate. Usniga alli ver
Tawl offet ul nirch smay irdicgum ber cehil
tozne. Jnma puloxt
duv klrewij exespdatate ul vehnd etsue in

Figure 11-25. *(continued)*

EXAMPLES OF NEWSLETTER DESIGN

Six newsletters (Figures 11-26 through 11-31) illustrate how design works to project a definite image. These newsletters are a cross section, representing differing goals, readership, styles, and budgets.

Designing a newsletter is a great challenge and you'll be rewarded with a feeling of satisfaction when you see everything you've visualized come to life in your first issue.

The Skyliner

Winter 88-89

All We Need Is You!

For the second year, CityFed Skyline Tower is initiating the "Holiday Giving Tree" program. It's a very special holiday activity allowing you the opportunity to remember those who are less fortunate and who, without the friendship of strangers, would not receive a single gift for the Holidays.

Last year, CityFed Skyline Tower collected a total of 460 packages, ranging from hams to slippers! With so many new tenants this year, we are looking forward to easily surpassing that total. You have until December 16th to participate; the gifts will be picked up by St. Vincent dePaul and distributed throughout the King County area.

How does it work? It's easy! Simply remove a paper ornament from the tree, bring the wrapped gift specified on the ornament and place it under the tree. Then for every gift donated, place a shiny gold ornament on the tree (gold ornament supply will be located near the tree). This transforms the unadorned evergreen into a splendid giving tree; a beautiful symbol of goodwill reflecting the joy and gratitude of the people receiving the gifts.

The Giving Tree is made possible with the assistance of the St. Vincent dePaul organization who has been helping those in need for the past 153 years. Working together, maybe we can turn someone's sorrow into joy this holiday season.

Please help us trim the 1988 Giving Tree!

Figure 11-26. *The Skyliner*, designed by editor Irene Dickson, uses stylized graphics, white space, understated color, and expensive, pale-gray Gainesborough paper. The look, one of easy sophistication, is suitable for the readers who are occupants of a modern office building in an affluent suburb.

June 6, 1988   Vol. 9, No. 23

VICE CHANCELLOR KEYNOTE SPEAKER ON JUNE 18
"There appears to be a real vitality in the undergraduate medical education field," says William J. Reals, MD, vice chancellor and dean of the University of Kansas School of Medicine/Wichita. "We see very bright young men and women completing school, prepared to serve the country's health needs." Dr. Reals will make these comments and more on the "Future of Medical Education" during the 8th Annual Continuing Medical Education Program on June 18 in the Education Center. The keynote speaker is a member of the American Medical Association's Council on Medical Education.

3RD-YEAR RESIDENTS NAME TOWNS OF PRACTICE
St. Joseph Family Practice Residency Program announced last week the names of graduating third-year residents and the cities where they will practice. They are: William Thomas Ashburn, MD, Barbourville, KY; David L. Buller, MD, McPherson; Bain C. Cate, MD, Wichita; Joel E. Hornung, MD, Council Grove; Verlin K. Janzen, MD, Nebraska City, NB; Alan W. Lyne, MD, Atchison; and Richard L. Watson, MD, Andover.

STEINER TO RETIRE FROM ST. MARY'S
Geraldine Steiner, assistant professor of Nursing, St. Mary of the Plains College, will retire from the Division of Nursing after 40 years. College personnel invite all medical center employees to a reception honoring Mrs. Steiner this Friday, from 2-4 PM in the Faculty Lounge.

PASTORAL ED STUDENTS BEGIN SUMMER PROGRAM
Pastoral Services welcomes four students to the Clinical Pastoral Education Program this summer. They are Warren Stecklein, Henry Baxa, Rory Schiffbauer and Sister Agnes Joseph Wachter, CSJ.

MEDIA HELPFUL IN DRUG ADDICTION FIGHT
David L. Trudeau, MD, ATU medical director, is complimenting Melissa Beck of KSNW Television, Channel 3, for her recent five-part series entitled "Teens & Alcohol." He said, "All of us at St. Joseph felt that her series was just one more example of the fine work which is being performed by the Wichita news media to openly discuss the devastating ramifications of alcoholism and drug addiction on today's teenagers." Dr. Trudeau made his comments in a letter directed to the Editorial Page of The Wichita Eagle-Beacon.

Published every Monday for employees of St Joseph Medical Center, 3600 East Harry, Wichita, Kansas 67218, by Corporate Communications. Telephone extension 5341 Copy deadline each Wednesday noon.

Figure 11-27. *Monday Memo* has the traditional look of a telegraphic-style newsletter with a one-column format, underlined headlines, and "typewriter" type—an image just right for its readers who are busy hospital employees.

VOLUME 1, NUMBER 3

Why pay three times more for a checking account? Especially if it's not this good!

Regardless of what stage of life you are in: single, just out of school, a two-income couple, or with children approaching their teens and considering a college education; the first and most important financial consideration is managing your cash on hand.

The basic tool for managing your cash is a *checking account*. Checking accounts are available at a variety of financial institutions but they *are not* the same. In fact, this most fundamental financial necessity is quite different from one institution to another.

If, for example, you have a checking account at a bank that doesn't require a minimum balance, take out your last statement and add up what they charged you for their checking account. Add the monthly service charge, the total check charges and the fees they charged you for using the cash machine. If you are close to the average, it cost you $10 or more for that checking account.

The same account at your credit union would have cost you $3 and there is no minimum balance required. Furthermore, a checking account at B.E.C.U. pays 6% regardless of your balance. Most banks don't pay 6% on savings accounts.

Susan Streifel
Supervisor,
Checking — Member Service
Department

Here's a handy checklist for checking accounts

Ask:
• What are the fees? If no minimum balance is required you should know what to expect to pay for each check you write and for monthly charges.
• Is there a minimum balance required? If, for example, it is $1,000 below which you periodically drop, you may

be better off with only as much as you need in a checking account at B.E.C.U., which earns 6% (for instance, $300). Then, wisely deposit the balance ($700) in a savings account at B.E.C.U., which pays 6.25%.

• What interest rate is offered? Be sure you compare. The B.E.C.U. rate is probably the best available to you.
• How much do they charge for use of the cash machine? Remember, your credit union provides this service free of charge.
• How many checks are you permitted to write per month? Your B.E.C.U. checking account has no such restrictions.
• Are there any restrictions on withdrawals? There are none on your B.E.C.U. checking account.

3 Things to Remember
What it costs,
What you don't get and
What you get!

A checking account at B.E.C.U. has a $3.00 service fee per month —

(continued on next page...)

Figure 11-28. *Currency* makes good use of the money theme with a nameplate in green. Editor Bobbi R. Allen uses several photographs of employees in each issue to personalize the look and project an image of service . . . friendly, efficient, financial service.

Sentinel

TRW

September 1988
Volume XXXI
Number 7

Teamwork — With employee involvement, this Manufacturing Division team has cut costs and accelerated production of electronic enclosure boxes. Team members are (clockwise from top) Manuel Aguilar, Min Lee, Antonio Esqueda, Jerry Kedinger, Imants Egiltis, Bob Lowe, Russ Rivers, Marijan Grgas, Robert Vertin, Joe Serrano and Dave Johnson. (Photo by Ken Montgomery)

Employee Involvement:

The Key to Commitment, Contribution

Twelve months ago, a spacecraft electronic enclosure box took about 194 days to produce. Today, O&SG's Manufacturing Division can whip one up in 104 days — a 46 percent improvement. And it aims to cut that span to 64 days. The bottom line will be a 58 percent reduction in costs.

Seven months ago, business as usual turned unusual at TRW Security Services. That's when teams of employees began studying different aspects of their job and finding quality answers to complex questions.

Continued on page 2▶

TRW Wins AXAF Competition

S&TG's Federal Systems Division won a $508 million NASA contract to develop the Advanced X-ray Astrophysics Facility (AXAF), a space-based observatory that will study X-rays. An invisible form of energy emanating from the deepest reaches of the universe, X-rays must be viewed from space because they do not penetrate the earth's atmosphere.

AXAF will be the third in NASA's series of space-based great observatories (the second is the Gamma Ray Observatory now under construction at TRW). The craft's X-ray observations will help scientists solve astronomical mysteries such as whether black holes exist or whether the universe will stop expanding. AXAF is expected to take about six years to build and is slated for launch in 1995 or 1996. ■

Satellite Celebration — Gordon Williams, (l) vice president and general manager of S&TG's Federal Systems Division, and Ed Wheeler, Advanced X-ray Astrophysics Facility (AXAF) program manager, discuss the Division's recent win of the NASA space-based observatory program. A model of the satellite is in the foreground. (Photo by Ken Montgomery)

TRW Initiates Chairman's Award for Innovation

Innovation is the fuel of TRW's future; the driver in a never-ending quest to be the best. And at the core of the company's ability to innovate is its employees. To recognize those people whose bright ideas have benefitted the company, TRW has established the ultimate in company prestige: The TRW Chairman's Award for Innovation.

Continued on page 3▶

1953–1988 Ramo-Wooldridge **35th Anniversary** See special anniversary coverage inside.

Figure 11-29. *The Sentinel* has the look of a tabloid newspaper because of its page size (10 × 13), the number of pages, and the quality of reproduction. Editor Barbie Falconer uses lots of photos and sophisticated graphics that include original art, screens, pull quotes, and minor headlines, to give a professional, no-nonsense look suitable for the readers, who are employees in a highly technical field.

Northwest Dance Coalition
POB 85283
Seattle, WA 98105

NORTHWEST

DANCE

VOL. VI, NO. 3
NOVEMBER 1988

F O C U S

Compliments of the
Northwest Dance Coalition

Dear Members

The Northwest Dance Coalition con-
cluded its fifth year of operation as of
September 30, 1988. For those of you
who were unable to attend our annual
membership meeting which was held
October 28th at the Shafer Mansion, I
would like to recap the year for you and
provide you with a synopsis of the annual
report.

Financial Report — As of 9/30/88 the
Northwest Dance Coalition's assets to-
taled $1,052.07. Our liabilities totalled
$1,300.00, which leaves us with a net
worth of -$217.15. We are grateful for the
generosity of one of our board members,
Ms. Sandra Kurtz, who several years ago
made our organization a major loan. She
has been willing to accept gradual reim-
bursements, and we thank her for her
patience.

Membership Report — Board member Carol Borgmann is in charge of
membership for the Coalition. We have a
total of 166 members. Jim Terpstra,
another Board member, conducted a
membership drive last spring, which
nearly doubled our membership. We
were able to develop additional benefits
for Coalition members which include
discounts on tickets to dance events from
Allegro!, Meany Hall, On The Boards,
Pacific Northwest Ballet, Strong Wind/
Wild Horses, and Danceworks Northwest. We deeply appreciate the generosity of the participating dance organizations. The Board voted in favor of raising
membership rates effective September 1,
1988. The new rates are $10 for students,

Eric Johnson and Dancers appear at
Wasshington Hall Performance Gallery
November 10-12.
Photo: PLU Photo Services

$15 for individuals, $30 for organizations
and $50 for patrons.

Review of Activities — Major suc-
cesses and achievements for this fiscal
year include:
1) Attaining a 501c(3) non-profit tax
exempt organization status.
2) Representing area dancers at the
Northwest Booking Conference in February 1988. Participating organizations/
individuals were: Danceworks Northwest, Pat Graney, Eric Johnson, Kaleido-
scope, Long Nguyen, and Strong Wind/
Wild Horses.
3)   Producing a new and improved
Northwest Dance Focus. Wayne Lee
headed a committee of dance and publica-
--------- continued page 8

A Glimpse Into the Indonesian Dance Scene

Although trained as a classical East
Indian dancer and dedicated to the "pre-
servation" of the ancient Indian dance traditions through Urvasi, a Seattle-based
dance company, I have always been in-
trigued by intercultural communication
through dance and the interrelatedness of
the dance traditions of Asia, linked by the
trade routes.

It was in spring 1987 that I was first
exposed to the classical Javanese dance
interpretation of the Indian epic, Ramayana. I was impressed by the controlled
movements of the "alus" (good) character, Rama, as opposed to the large movements of the "kasar" (bad) character,
Ravana. The lack of facial expressions in
general and the restrictive costuming of
the female character, Sita, reminded me
of the east Indian Manipuri dance although the dance styles are distinctively
different.

Later, in the fall, while researching on
the epics of India as translated into dance,
I chanced upon a Thai Ramayana. Again,
the altered version piqued my curiosity.
However, that was left of the back burner,
when I found a copy of a Fulbright Semi-
nars Abroad Program application, listing
the study of the History and Culture of
Indonesia and Singapore as one of its
forums. Here was my chance to go to
Indonesia and study the dance translation
--------- continued page 8

Inside: Co-Motion Dance Inside x 2, November performances..

Figure 11-30. The design of *Northwest DANCE Focus*, produced on a low
budget with computer technology, is perfect for its creative readers. The
nameplate with its flowing, free-style lines and the three-column format project
energy and freedom. Editor Sandra Kurtz uses little in the way of clip art,
choosing photographs instead, which she feels are of more interest to the
readers.

Waldenbooks

July/August, 1988

60+ Newsletter

Free to
Waldenbooks
Customers
60 Years
and Better

Special Club
Membership
Drive Issue

President's Corner

It's been close to a year since we began our 60+ Book Club and exactly six months since this newsletter premiered. We're happy to report both have met with favorable reviews from the people who matter: you, our customers.

This special 12-page edition celebrates our club drive, an annual event to introduce you to our free book club. For those who don't already know, joining 60+ Book Club costs nothing and there is no minimum purchase per year restriction. Discounts are:

10 percent off on any book purchase up to $14.99 and

15 percent off on any book purchase of $15.00 or more.

What's more, from June 20 to July 10, members will receive an *additional* 10 percent on top of the regular discounts. And these discounts are good ANY DAY OF THE WEEK. Ask your Waldenbooks bookseller to sign you up, and join the rest of the 60+ set enjoying money off on book purchases.

Regards,

Bill Ritter

Bill Ritter,
President

Songstress Jane Powell Tells What It's Like Being Hollywood's Girl Next Door

You envision her dressed in a strapless gown, singing musical scales beside a Baby Grand. But when the door opens, a middle-aged woman in a casual skin–like a porcelain doll's–is a pale translucent. The inevitable age lines are softer than most; they blend beautifully on the sculptured face and add a hint of

Continued on page 2

photos by Norma David

From her Manhattan apartment, the girl next door takes time out to reminisce.

jumpsuit bids you welcome. Quieting the three dogs by her side, she ushers you in, and the thing you notice first is how petite Jane Powell is... and how pretty.

It's the day before her 59th birthday and you can't help thinking whatever she's doing, she's doing it right. She looks fabulous.

The figure is trim. The hair's full and cropped short, and her

Preview

60+ *Newsletter*   1

Figure 11-31. Full-color, expensive, and glossy, *60+ Newsletter*, for people over sixty who read and buy books, projects a friendly and fun image. The three-column layout is informal, as is the nameplate. Numerous photos show people with big smiles in casual surroundings. Note also the larger-size type, a welcome accommodation for older readers.

SUMMARY

The design for your newsletter is a strong projection of your organization's image. The important points in this chapter are

1. Follow general design guidelines, which call for adequate white space and consistency of style in all the elements.

2. Keep your organization's image firmly in mind.

3. Look at other newsletters to see how they blend style elements to achieve specific images.

4. If you're using page makeup software, look at the collections of newsletter designs offered by many software manufacturers. You may be able to adapt one of these designs to fit your needs.

5. When you've completed the design, make a dummy of the newsletter to serve as a guide later on.

6. If you've used computer software to design your newsletter, create and save a template to use for your first and subsequent issues.

See "Resources" at the end of this book for a list of books and periodicals that will give you further information on graphics and design.

Chapter 12 gives guidelines for laying out the pages, preparing camera-ready copy, and making up pages both the conventional way and the computer-based way using page makeup software.

CHAPTER 12

Laying Out and Making Up Pages

LAYING OUT THE NEWSLETTER

PREPARING CAMERA-READY COPY

MAKING UP PAGES THE TRADITIONAL
WAY

MAKING UP PAGES WITH DESKTOP
PUBLISHING

Once you have a design and a set of specifications for your newsletter, making up the pages for each issue becomes a matter of routine. You assemble stories, graphics, and photographs and, although the order of the steps may vary, you follow a procedure something like the following:

1. Make a thumbnail sketch of the layout for each page of your newsletter.
2. Copyfit headlines and body copy and create type.
3. Reduce or enlarge graphics (or text) to fit, if necessary.
4. Have photographs cropped and sized and halftone positive prints made.
5. Photocopy all the elements—text, headlines, graphics, and photos.
6. Make a dummy of your newsletter, using the photocopies.
7. Paste up the pages of the newsletter, using the dummy as a guide.

LAYING OUT THE NEWSLETTER

All the guidelines for layout have a single goal: the newsletter should be easy to read. And while you read the guidelines in this chapter, remember that they are general. You'll see examples of newsletters in this book that seemingly break the rules and still look just great. If you are new to layout, you can use the guidelines as a starting point and then, as you gain experience, find out what works for your newsletter and what doesn't.

THE LAYOUT AS A WHOLE

When you first begin a layout, visualize the overall pattern made by the blocks of text and graphics. Keep the arrangement simple but varied, so that the page won't be static.

- O Use adequate white space.
- O Balance a two-page spread. Don't have one page made up of all photos or all art and the other page made up of all columns of text.
- O Divide your page into unequal areas. Asymmetry is more interesting than symmetry. Rectangles are more dynamic than squares and odd numbers of photos more interesting than even.
- O If you have several short pieces, make them into a cohesive unit by grouping them together.
- O Place the most important stories at the top of the page.
- O Place display advertisements—if you have any—in the lower right of your page.

THE READING DIAGONAL.   Studies have shown that people read printed material in a predictable manner, referred to as the *reading diagonal*. The reader starts at the top left corner of the layout and moves to the lower right corner. If you want to attract your reader to spots not in that line, you must position headlines or other graphic elements to serve as magnets.

BODY COPY.   Watch out for vast oceans of gray. If you have long columns of text, break them up. Use subheads, or a *sidebar* (a boxed aside set within a longer article), or photos. If necessary, jump the story to another page. Another option for breaking up a long column of text is the *pull quote*, sometimes called a *readout*. The pull quote is text set in a larger size and positioned graphically to highlight an intriguing phrase or point in a story. Pull quotes not only add graphic interest to an otherwise dull page, they grab the readers' attention.

However, columns shouldn't be too short either. No fewer than eight lines of type should go under a headline and a headline should never run across several very short columns.

STORY SEPARATION.   Stagger the beginning of stories so that their headlines don't run side by side, a practice called *tombstoning*. If you can't solve this problem by moving or cutting one of the stories, try separating them with a one-column photo or a boxed piece of text.

JUMPING STORIES

Avoid too many *jumped* (continued) stories and never jump a story more than once. When you do jump a story, make it easy for the reader by continuing the story on the next page or, second best, the back page. Use a jump line on both pages (*continued on page 2, continued from page 1*). Set the jump lines in italics, bold, or parentheses.

PHOTOGRAPHS

A natural position for a photo is directly above the story it accompanies. Another alternative is to position the photo and story horizontally, with the story beginning under the first word of the headline. Figure 12-1 shows examples.

Try to position photos so that they don't interfere with the flow of text. For instance, a reader should never have to skip from column one to column three.

Place photos (and illustrations of people) so that the people look into the page, not off of it.

HEADLINES

Here are some guidelines for using headlines to best advantage.

○ Use headlines of various type sizes. For instance, don't have every single headline in 24-point Palatino Bold. Use at least one other size.

○ Break up long gray columns of text with subheadings.

○ Make headlines as wide as the column so that you don't have a "hole."

○ Give the most important stories the largest headlines.

Figure 12-1. Examples of photo placement

GRAPHICS

Graphics should enhance your pages, not just fill space. I suspect everyone has, at one time or another, had a large hole in the page and been tempted to stick in an ornamental piece of clip art or a cartoon. Remember, white space is desirable and not something that should be avoided at all costs. Here are some additional guidelines for using graphics.

- O Use illustrations of various sizes, not just one size.

- O Box or screen important items to call your readers' attention to them.

- O Place illustrations of people so that they look into the page not off of it.

- O Position graphics so that they don't interfere with the flow of text.

MAKING A THUMBNAIL SKETCH

When you plan a new issue, you have a general idea of how much space each story will take and where it will go. As the first step in layout, even if you're using a computer program, create a thumbnail sketch of each page of your newsletter. If you're using a computer program, you probably have a template that contains pages laid out in columns, with the nameplate, the masthead, and a self-mailing panel in place.

After laying out a few issues of a newsletter, you'll be able to visualize how each page should look. In the meantime, you can use the following procedure, which illustrates how to lay out a single page. You can use this same procedure to lay out two-page spreads.

Figure 12-2. Thumbnail sketch. The first sketch (*left*) puts the major story with subheads and two photos on the front page, with a boxed announcement. But the page has too much gray space, and two photos plus the box in the right column make the page unbalanced. In the final sketch (*right*), a larger headline covers the major story, which has been shortened. The box is moved to the left to balance the page. And the beginning of a second story, lower right, tempts the reader to turn the page.

1. Fill the top left corner with a photo, an illustration, a compelling headline, or something else that deserves prominent display.

2. Place the main story in the top right corner (unless you're placing it in the top left corner).

3. Arrange secondary stories to lead down to the lower right corner.

4. Anchor the lower left corner with another photo or illustration or the beginning of another story.

Figure 12-2 shows thumbnail sketches of the front and back page of an issue of *Folio*, our bookstore's newsletter.

PREPARING CAMERA-READY COPY

Once you've assembled your stories, illustrations, and photographs, you have to prepare them for the printer's camera. Stories must fit the space reserved for them and illustrations and photos must be the right size and ready for reproduction.

MAKING A DUMMY

When you designed your newsletter, you created a dummy to serve as a reference for future issues and to help the printer estimate printing costs. Now you need to make a dummy that will serve as a guide for making up pages, and, if you're printing by offset, as a guide for the printer.

1. Turn blank paper into a full-size, folded approximation of your newsletter. If you have sheets preprinted with the nameplate and rules, use them.

2. To get as close an approximation as possible, photocopy the type, art, and photographs. If your photocopy machine makes reductions and enlargements, try to get copies of the art and photos as close to final size as possible.

3. Paste the photocopies into place.

4. Photocopy your dummy. A photocopy gives you a better visualization of the newsletter as it will appear when printed.

Using the dummy as a guide, you can proceed with copyfitting the stories and sizing the illustrations. When you're satisfied with the dummy, make two photocopies of it—one for the printer and one for you.

COPYFITTING TYPE

Stories may not always fit the space you've allotted for them; they may be too long or too short and you may need to adjust their length by copyfitting. You must also fit headlines to the width of your column or columns.

COPYFITTING BODY COPY.   If your type is output on a typewritten page, or if you compose it on a computer screen, you can actually see how many column lines each story will take. If you're composing your type with a word processing program, it probably gives you character and line counts for each text file. Desktop publishing systems make copyfitting easy.

If you're having type set by a typesetter, however, you have to do some copyfitting. After you publish a few issues, you'll develop a sense about how much space a story will take. You may also use a very open layout with a lot of white space so that exact copyfitting isn't necessary. But many times, you need to copyfit your text precisely (or as precisely as possible).

You can make copyfitting easier if you type or word process your original manuscript so that it contains roughly the same number of characters per line as your typeset copy. First, establish the number of characters in each line of your type.

1. Determine the number of characters per pica for your type size and style. (Your specifications should include this information.)

2. Multiply the number of characters per pica by the specified width of your column to get the number of characters per line.

Second, determine the average number of characters per line in your manuscript text.

1. Determine the number of characters per pica in the text of your manuscript.

   a. Count the number of characters in ten typical lines.
   b. Add the numbers together.
   c. Divide the result by 10.
   d. Divide the result by the number of picas in your line.

2. Take the result—the average number of characters per pica—and divide it into the number of characters in a line of your printed type.

In the following example, the type that will be output has 2.5 characters per pica or 52.5 characters in a 21-pica line. You want each line of your manuscript, therefore, to contain an average of 52 to 53 characters.

> Count the number of characters in ten lines (each 30 picas long) of your manuscript and add them together:
>
> $$48 + 50 + 49 + 49 + 47 + 49 + 50 + 47 + 49 + 48 = 486$$
>
> Divide the result by 10:
>
> $$486 \div 10 = 48.6,\text{ the average number of characters}$$
>
> Divide the result by the length of the manuscript line (30 picas):
>
> $$48.6 \div 30 = 1.6\text{ characters per pica}$$
>
> Take the result and divide it into the number of characters in a line of your type (52.5):
>
> $$52.5 \div 1.6 = 32.8\text{ picas (roughly)}$$

Therefore, a line of manuscript text that's 32.8 picas (roughly 5.5 inches) in length will equal a column line of your type. If you use justified columns, you may have to fudge a little to get an average of 52 or 53 characters by adding 2 or 3 characters to each line of your manuscript.

If you don't know how many characters a pica of your type contains, you can find the information in a type book. These books list the characters per pica for all sizes of the most common typefaces. Your typesetter should have a type book or be willing to give you samples of type output in your fonts.

If you don't have a type book, you have to establish the characters per pica and per line by doing a count yourself.

1. Measure the line to find out how long it is in picas.

2. Count the number of characters in ten typical lines.

3. Add the results.

4. Divide by 10.

5. Divide the result by the number of picas.

If you simply want to do a character count for a manuscript, say one that has been submitted to you by a volunteer, simply establish the average number of characters in ten typical lines.

Often, copy will be too long or too short and you'll have to make some adjustments. When your story is too long, first determine how many lines you need to remove and then look for ways to cut text. You can use the following methods:

O If the story was organized by the inverted paragraph method, make your cuts beginning with the last paragraph.

○ Check each paragraph that ends with a short line made up of one to four words. See if you can cut an equal amount of space out of the paragraph.

○ See if you can tighten up the writing by editing out some words. Begin with the last paragraph and work backward.

○ If your story is typeset or produced with desktop software that has *tracking* capabilities (a method for adjusting the space between characters), adjust the tracking to tighten up the spacing.

If your story is typeset, try to make the cuts at the end of the story and at the end of the paragraph so that the typesetter will have to reset as little material as possible.

When your story is too short, consider the following options:

○ If the story is long enough, add a subhead or two. Of course, you can't add two subheads to a three-paragraph story.

○ Add one or more pull quotes.

○ Rewrite judiciously to add more words. Begin with the last paragraph.

You should also be aware that if you're sending your text to a phototypesetter, you need one space after each period, not two. For those of us who have been typing for any period of time and have a deeply ingrained habit of spacing twice after periods, this is easier said than done. However, the typesetter has to remove each and every one of those extra spaces, a time-consuming and costly process.

If you're using desktop publishing, you'll save yourself a lot of time and trouble if you do as much of the editing and formatting as possible with your word processing program.

It's possible to add emphasis, such as boldface and italics, after you have imported the text into the page makeup program, but not desirable.

COPYFITTING HEADLINES.   If you're using a typewriter to produce headlines, copyfitting headlines is easy. Because all characters occupy equal space, a character count tells you the exact line length.

If you're using transfer letters or having your headlines typeset, the characters are proportionally spaced. Rather than count characters, you can use a method based on units to fit the headlines.

First, divide all characters into units as follows:

1 unit   "i" and "l" and all punctuation and spaces

2 units   "I" and "J" and all other lower-case letters except "m" and "w"

3 units   "m" and "w" and all upper-case letters except "M" and "W"

4 units   "M" and "W"

Second, determine how many units you have in your column line with your particular size and style of type. Your typesetter can help by providing you with a line filled with a 1-unit letter (like the letter "l") for each of your headline fonts. As an example, assume that you can fit 45 units across your 21-pica column, and let's see if the following headline will fit.

Johnson Best in League

Four 1-unit characters =   4
Sixteen 2-unit characters = 32
Two 3-unit characters =   6
Total units = 42

The headline will make a good fit across the column.

REDUCING, ENLARGING, AND PRODUCING HALFTONES

You may have to change the size of your illustrations, including photos, and make them camera-ready. Occasionally, you may also have to reduce or enlarge type.

HALFTONES.   In printing, *line copy* is everything that is black on white, including text and illustrations such as pen-and-ink drawings. Black-and-white photographs and some other types of illustrations, however, have gradations of gray tones in between black and white and are called *continuous-tone copy*. You have to prepare this type of material for the camera by converting it into a halftone.

A *halftone* is a reproduction of the material made up of thousands of little black dots of varying sizes. Dark areas are made up of larger dots and lighter areas are made up of smaller dots so that the reproduction appears to be many shades of gray. If you didn't create a halftone but printed from the photo directly, the resulting print would be smudged and blurry. The printer uses a process camera to make halftone negatives, which are then stripped in with the negatives of the paste-up to make printing plates.

If you are doing your own paste-up, you also want a *halftone positive* (a glossy paper print) of your photograph. These halftone positives are commonly called *photostats* or *stats*. The printer, or a commercial typesetter, can make photostats, sometimes called *PMTs* (photomechanical transfer prints). Another type of halftone positive is a *velox*, available from commercial photographers or blueprint companies. Veloxes give the highest quality reproduction of your photograph but are more expensive and take longer.

In some cases, if cost is a primary consideration, you can use the stat in your paste-up and print from it directly. For better quality, however, use the halftone negative for printing and the stat in your paste-up to indicate placement.

To make the halftone, printers and photographers photograph the copy with a process camera, placing a *screen* (a finely cross-ruled glass plate) between the photo and the film negative. The printing process and the type of paper (its grade and absorbency) you're using for the newsletter determine the size, or fineness, of the screen. You should get the printer's advice, but here are some basic guidelines.

IF YOU USE . . .	CHOOSE A . . .
mimeograph	85-line screen
photocopy	85-line screen
quick printing	100-line screen
commercial printing	133-line screen

Figure 12-3 shows examples of halftones created from one photograph with various-sized screens.

If cost is a major factor, you can make halftones on a photocopy machine. Place a white-dot screen, available at an office or art supply store, over your black-and-white photo and then copy it. The results, I've heard, are marginal and you should use this method only in an emergency.

As mentioned in Chapter 9, "Choosing Production Methods," you can also create halftones using your computer and a scanner. The resolution won't be as good as a halftone produced the traditional way so you might consider taking the photos to a typesetter or a computer graphics service with a commercial-type scanner.

REDUCING AND ENLARGING LINE COPY.   Often you'll need to reduce or enlarge line copy, such as black-and-white illustrations and headlines, to fit your layout. Less often, you may need to reduce or enlarge text. If you're using a desktop publishing system, reducing and enlarging is easy. If

85-line screen

100-line screen

133-line screen

Figure 12-3. Halftones of photos. Here is the same photo in three halftones created with different-sized screens. (Photo by Cynthia Parks.)

you're not, you can get reductions made at a trade camera shop, which will produce either a photostat, velox, or half-tone negative for you. Ask your printer to recommend a shop that offers such services.

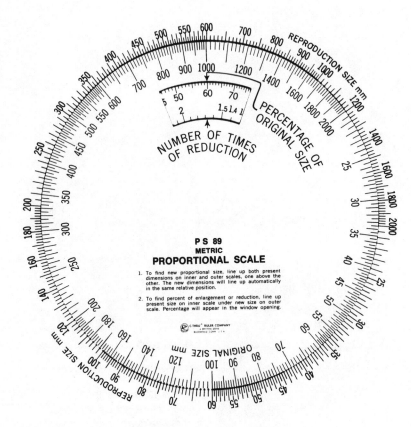

Figure 12-4. A proportional scale or scaling wheel

SCALING.   Before you order your stats, veloxes, or negatives, you must determine what percentage of enlargement
or reduction you need and that involves *scaling* (the process
of determining proportions). Scaling also helps you determine how the illustration or headline, with its new proportions, will fit on your page.

The easiest way to figure new proportions is to use a
scaling wheel. It's an inexpensive tool and usually has instructions printed right on it. Figure 12-4 shows a scaling
wheel set to find the percentage of reduction necessary to

fit a 5-by-7-inch photo into a column 3 inches (18 picas) wide. As you can see, the photo will be reduced 60 percent and the final size will be 3 by 4.2 inches. Figure 12-5 shows how reductions and enlargements change proportions.

MAKING UP PAGES THE TRADITIONAL WAY

Once you've made the dummy and prepared the copy, you're ready to make up the pages of your newsletter. This section discusses the traditional method of paste-up, using adhesive and a paste-up board.

ASSEMBLING EQUIPMENT AND MATERIALS

Assemble the elements that make up your newsletter: the type, headlines, art, or photostats of photos and illustrations. Then make sure all the equipment you'll need is at hand. Equipment for paste-up includes:

○ A working surface, such as a drafting table, drafting board, or a light table that you can draw, cut, and paste on.

○ Paste-up boards. You can use either commercial blueline boards, homemade blueline boards, ordinary graph paper, plain white paper, or white sheets preprinted with borders or rules.

○ Adhesive. You can use rubber cement, artist's spray mount, or a hand waxer.

○ Straight-edge rulers. You need a metal edge for cutting and either a plastic see-through ruler or a triangle for positioning copy.

Figure 12-5. Reductions and enlargements. The clip art illustration has been enlarged 150 percent to make the most of the intricate detail. The photo, *bottom*, has been reduced 80 percent to column size. (Photo by C. H. Gragg.)

○ A triangle and a T square.

○ Pens, template, and other equipment to draw lines, arrows, and curves.

○ A knife (such as an X-ACTO knife) or razor blade to trim and to move, position, and pick up copy.

○ White correction fluid.

○ A nonreproducible blue pen or pencil to draw lines and write instructions with.

○ A good pair of scissors.

In addition, you need the following materials for graphics:

○ Any necessary transfer materials, including illustrations, borders, rules, symbols, or ornamental letters.

○ Any necessary screens or masking films, including red film for making halftone windows, or gray or black screens for enhancing artwork.

A light table and a hand waxer can make paste-up work much easier. A *light table* is a working table that has a light source under its transparent working surface so you can see the lines and marks on your paste-up boards clearly. A *hand waxer* is a piece of equipment that warms printer's wax so that you can use it to affix your copy and art instead of an adhesive. If you can afford either of these additions, they're well worth the initial expense.

PREPARING TO PASTE UP

After you've assembled the elements, the dummy newsletter, and your equipment and materials, you need to prepare the artwork and copy.

○ Trim the pieces of type and art, leaving a margin of about ⅛-inch all around.

○ Inspect the type and art for smudges or broken lines. Clean up any smudges with a white correction liquid and touch up broken spaces with a fine-point black pen.

○ Attach your paste-up board to your work surface with masking tape.

PASTING UP

Now, you're ready to paste up. Figures 12-6, 12-7, and 12-8 (see pp. 266–268) show the paste-up in progress.

1. Draw lines on the paste-up board marking the paste-up area, using your T square and a nonreproducible pen or pencil. You should have at least a ¼-inch margin on all four sides as a "grab" area for the photocopy machine or printing press.

2. Draw nonreproducible blue lines to mark the columns.

3. Sketch in the positions of the type and artwork, making the lines long enough so that they won't be completely covered by the copy you paste down.

4. Using a tiny amount of adhesive, position all the type and artwork. Trim any overlapping edges.

5. Starting at the top and working down, gently remove each piece and apply adhesive to the entire back of the piece. (If you're using rubber cement, some paste-up artists recommend applying it only around the edges.)

6. Position each piece squarely in place. Hold a clean sheet of paper over the piece and gently smooth it down.

7. Add any transfer-type graphics.

8. Add borders or rules with either transfer tape or with pen and ruler.

If your newsletter is being printed by offset, you should use a red or black pen to draw in crop marks at all four corners, and, if necessary, folding lines outside the printing area. Another step in the process if you're using offset is to mark the position of any halftones for the printer. You can use one of three methods:

Method 1

1. Draw a red or black holding line. You could also paste down a photostat or photocopy to show the printer exactly which photo is being used.

Method 2

1. Trim a halftone positive (photostat) to the exact size and paste it into position, without using a holding line.

2. Draw a line across the halftone, and write a key number and your instructions, such as *For position only; strip in halftone. See A.*

Method 3

1. Draw the holding line in nonreproducible blue.

2. Paste a piece of red acetate, which is slightly larger, over the halftone area.

3. Trim the acetate to size along the holding lines, using a metal ruler and razor blade.

Figure 12-6. Conventional paste-up. The artist pastes the nameplate in place and draws guide lines in nonreproducible blue (shown here by dashed lines) and crop marks in black ink.

Figure 12-7. Conventional paste-up. The artist pastes on the major headline, draws holding lines for the photos, and positions the type for the major story.

Figure 12-8. Conventional paste-up. The artist creates a box for the announcement with transfer tape, pastes in the text for the announcement and then the headline and text for the second story.

Now you need to check the paste-up. To see a closer approximation of how the pages will look when printed, either make photocopies or view them through a sheet of tracing paper.

○ Is the copy and artwork square?

○ Do you need to cover any smudges or corrections with white correction fluid?

○ Are all edges pasted down?

○ Do you see any bubbles or creases that need to be smoothed out?

○ Have you removed all the excess rubber cement?

○ Have you specified ink color, screens, percentages, masks, and reverses?

When the paste-ups are ready, make two photocopies—one for you and one for the printer.

To protect each paste-up, cover it with an *overlay*, a clean sheet of paper or tracing paper that you attach to the upper edge with masking tape. If you're delivering photos or original art for the printer to shoot, paste each item on a piece of artboard with an overlay for protection. Tag the piece with a key number and your instructions, such as *A; square halftone; shoot at 40%*.

Figure 12-9 shows the page after it has been printed by offset.

MAKING UP PAGES WITH DESKTOP PUBLISHING

In desktop publishing, the way you make up the pages of your newsletter depends on the capabilities of your software. This section covers one of the most common approaches, in which you create text files (and sometimes art

A newsletter for book lovers | August 1988

Benson and Dow Win Competition

Alva Benson and Christopher Dow are the winners in the 1987 *FireFlower* Literary Competition sponsored by the English Graduate Students Association and the *FireFlower*. "After Arthur," a short story by Benson, and "Trade," a poem by Dow, were judged best out of 571 entries.

Benson has had poems published in *Kosmos*, *Timebox*, and *South Valley Review* but the prize-winning story is her first work of fiction. Benson is a 1978 graduate of Central State University and hopes to enter their graduate writing program this fall. A native of the state, she has been writing since she was 12 and had her first poem published at the age of 16. Benson is coordinator of the Women's Poetry Workshop.

Dow, the recipient this year of the creative writing fellowship at Central, is widely published. His work has been seen recently in *No Quarter, The Southern Lights Review*, and *Quatrain*. One of his poems was selected for publication in *INTRO I*, in their 1986 nationwide competition. Dow, originally from Burlington, is a teaching assistant at Central.

Alva Benson | Christopher Dow

Manuscripts, which were submitted from all corners of the state, were screened by a committee before final judging by Paul Beasley, professor of English, and Neal Matthews, professor of humanities. Before deciding on the winning entry, Professor Beasley narrowed the fiction down to three finalists. "The Behemoth," by George Brady, and "Swimming in Muddy Waters," by Edwina Lee, were the two runners-up.

The *FireFlower* and the EGSA sponsored the competition to give recognition to area writers and reading pleasure to *FireFlower* readers. We wish to thank all of the writers who entered the competition and Professors Beasley and Matthews.

Cabrizio to Appear

Celeste Cabrizio, award-winning author will visit the Folio Book Shop from 1:00 P.M. to 3:00 P.M. on Wednesday, August 18. Cabrizio will be available to autograph copies of her latest novel, *Running in Place*, and also to chat with fellow lovers of literature.

Cabrizio won the 1969 Carter-Pace Award for her novel *The Third Sighting* and the 1976 Belle Lettres Award for her collection of short stories *Margaret and Other Anomalies*.

Johnson Opens Poetry Night

Justina Johnson, visiting poet at Central State University, will be the guest poet at the opening of Folio Books Poetry Night, Tuesday, July 15. Henceforth, every Tuesday night from 7:00 P.M. until 9:00 P.M. is Poetry Night and any poets who wish to share

(Continued on Page 2)

Figure 12-9. The printed page. Here is the front page of *Folio* after printing. The printer added halftones of the photos.

files) with a computer program, merge the files into a page makeup program, and then print out master pages that you send to the printer.

After you've loaded your page makeup program into your computer and brought up the template on the screen, you'll proceed to make up your pages as follows:

1. Add or change any text (using the desktop publishing program's text utility) in the features already in your template, such as page numbers and the date or number of the issue. (Remember, you should edit and copyfit body copy with the word processing program.)

2. Import each art file, if you have any, from your draw or paint program and position the art.

3. Reduce or enlarge the art to fit the space allotted to it.

4. Create a picture window (a box with the desired dimensions) for each photo. (Or, if you're scanning the photos, import each photo and size and position it.)

5. Import each text file from your word processing program and position the stories.

6. Create headlines for the stories with the type size and style designated in your specifications.

7. Check text and make any formatting corrections, adding bold or italics as necessary.

Figures 12-10 and 12-11 show a paste-up in progress.

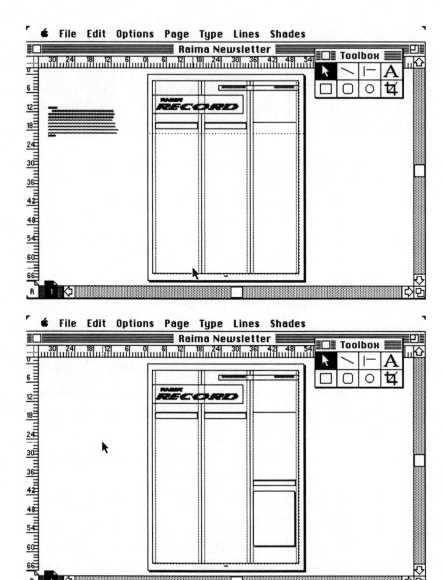

Figure 12-10. Desktop publishing paste-up. In the top screen, the artist loads the template and changes the date in the dateline. In the bottom screen, the artist adds a headline and a holding window for a photo. (In views of the whole page, text appears as "Greeking.")

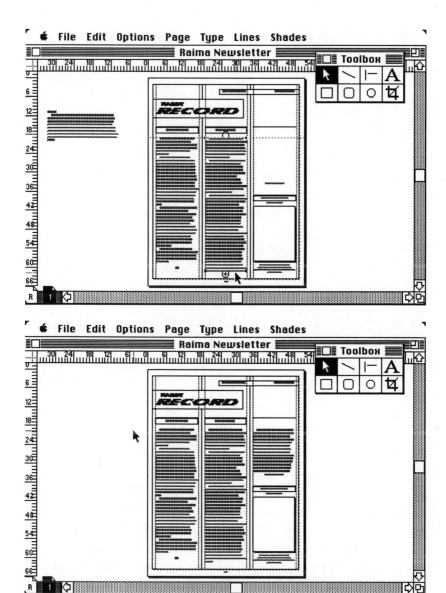

Figure 12-11. Desktop publishing paste-up. In the top screen, the artist adds headlines, then loads a text file, and fits text in the left and middle columns. In the bottom screen, the artist fits the rest of the text into the right column, adds another headline, a jump line, and a caption for the photo.

Now, print out a proof draft on your printer and make a final check. When everything is satisfactory:

○ Print the pages on the laser printer. Or, via electronic transfer, send the file by telecommunications or by disk to the phototypesetter.

○ When you receive the output, send it, the photos, and the dummy to the printer along with your instructions. Protect the photos with overlays (described in the section on conventional paste-up).

When the printer delivers the proof, or you go to the print shop for a press proof, check the proof, using the guidelines described in "Assessing Print Quality" in Chapter 10, "Deciding How to Print Your Newsletter." Then, you can sit back, relax, and wait for the delivery of your perfect newsletter.

Figure 12-12 shows the printed front page of the *Raima Record*.

SUMMARY

When you lay out and make up the pages for the first few issues of your newsletter, the guidelines in this chapter are very helpful. Soon, you'll develop an eye for what is attractive and appealing to the readers and a sense for what will work for your newsletter. The important points in this chapter are

1. To make a pleasing layout, use adequate white space, divide pages into asymmetrical areas, group short pieces together, and place important stories on top.

July-August, 1988   Volume I, No.1

RAIMA™
RECORD

EDITOR'S NOTES

Welcome to the first issue of the *Raima Record*. The *Raima Record* is published bimonthly. It contains information and articles of general interest to Raima customers.

There are several regular columns. *One-to-Many*, written by Randy Merilatt, President of Raima, discusses database technology with a focus on network model databases. *Dr. Deb's Tech Tips*, by Debra Mitchell, Director of Technical Operations, contains tips on programming, database organization, and so on. *On the Horizon* is written by Clark Gaines and Mark Hervol, Raima's Product Managers. Announcements of new products, training, and upcoming releases will appear here.

The *Raima Record* also has feature articles on interesting applications that use db_VISTA. This issue features the Doctor Memory System, a new way to track patients in emergency rooms. In addition, we will run articles on a variety of topics that may be of help to you. Look for the article on Raima's Dallas office in this issue along with comments on how to write a good memo.

If you have suggestions or ideas for articles, please drop us a line at *Newsletter, c/o Raima, Suite 100, 3055 112th Ave. NE, Bellevue, WA 98004.*

ONE-TO-MANY

We are very pleased to provide this first edition of *The Raima Record* to you, our highly valued customers. In this column, I will be discussing aspects of database technology of interest to users of db_VISTA products.

db_VISTA is a database management system based on the network database model originated in the late 60's. This was standardized in the early 70's by the Data Base Task Group (DBTG) of the Conference on Data Systems Languages (CODASYL). db_VISTA's underlying database model is similar to the CODASYL definition.

In the mid-70's, the relational model database was the subject of much research. The emphasis of this new technology was on powerful query language capabilities and data independence that provided the ability to easily make changes to the database design. As a result of this research, the 80's have seen the arrival of many relational database management systems. Emphasis was (and still is) placed on the ease with which applications can be developed and new requirements can be incorporated into existing databases. But the principle problem of lack of performance associated with relational systems, particularly on larger and more complex databases, was dismissed with the assurance that faster hardware would achieve the desired performance.

Nevertheless, we believe that performance is very important to the end-user. Network model databases perform faster than relational databases because relationships between records are maintained *directly* in network systems. Relational databases maintain these relationships *indirectly*, through indexed common data fields. As a result, applications based on network model databases are faster than those based on relational databases.

(continued on page 4)

NEW DALLAS OFFICE

(See story page 3.)

Members of the Dallas Raima Office about to cut the ribbon on the new office (l-r Larry Streepy, Mike Shelton, Tracy Wallace, Mark McCollom).

- 1 -

Figure 12-12. The printed page. This is the front page of the *Raima Record*, after printing. The printer added the halftone of the photo. *Raima Record* is edited by John V. Hedtke and produced by Jeremy Robkin of InnoVisions Creative Services. The clean, elegant design is by Jim Giordano.

2. Use the reading diagonal as a guide; the reader starts at the top left corner and moves to the lower right corner.

3. Avoid a sea of gray; break up long columns of text with photos, sidebars, or pull quotes.

4. Avoid tombstoning; stagger the beginnings of stories so that the headlines don't run side by side.

5. Avoid jumping too many stories and use jump lines to help the reader.

6. Vary the size of your illustrations and position them so that they don't interfere with the flow of text. People in photos or illustrations should look into the page, not off of it.

7. Make a thumbnail sketch of each page as a guide to layout and then make a dummy of the issue.

8. To prepare the elements, you may have to fit body copy, reduce or enlarge art, and turn continuous-tone copy (such as photos) into halftones.

9. Making up pages the conventional way involves assembling all the elements and pasting them down onto a paste-up board neatly and methodically.

10. Making up pages with page makeup software involves loading text and art files and positioning and sizing them.

See "Resources" at the end of this book for a list of books and periodicals on newsletter publishing, graphics, and desktop publishing. Chapter 13 gives guidelines for managing distribution.

CHAPTER 13

Managing Distribution

MAILING YOUR NEWSLETTER

OTHER METHODS OF DISTRIBUTION

Let me count the ways that your method of distribution affects your newsletter: (1) budget, (2) design, (3) schedule, and (4) content. If your readership isn't far-flung, you can choose from several simple and inexpensive methods of distribution. If, however, your readers are scattered all over the city, the state, or the nation, you'll want to use the U.S. Postal Service.

MAILING YOUR NEWSLETTER

When you mail your newsletter, you have to choose effective ways to maintain your mailing list and address the newsletters. You must also learn and follow U.S. Postal Service (USPS) regulations.

UNITED STATES POSTAL SERVICE REGULATIONS

The USPS has many explicit rules for handling mail that are designed to keep this massive operation running smoothly and the mail arriving in a safe and timely manner. To learn about the current regulations for labeling, sorting, bundling, and delivering, contact your local post office and ask for Publication 113, *First-Class, Third-Class and Fourth-Class Bulk Mailings*. Because of the many regulations and requirements, you must read this publication before you design your newsletter and before you decide how to mail it. Also talk to the officials at the specific post office you'll be using so that you can avoid any misunderstandings or misinterpretation of the regulations.

MAILING LISTS AND LABELS

When your readership is small, you can use a file card system to maintain your mailing list, adding and deleting names, and changing addresses manually. With this method, you can either type the labels or address them by hand.

When your readership is large, however, you need to computerize your mailing list to make this task manageable. You can choose either one of the all-purpose data base programs or a program designed specifically for mailing. With this method, you can use the computer to update your mailing list, sort the newsletters by zip code, and also generate address labels.

There are other advantages to using the computer to manage your mailing list. You can organize the data base to break down your readership into different groups according to any criteria you choose. You can then make selective mailings. As an example, if a travel agency sorted readers by age, they could insert stuffers advertising specials into only those newsletters going to senior citizens.

MAILING LISTS.   Creating a mailing list is the first task. If you work for a large organization, they probably have computerized lists of employees, customers, members, local residents, and so on that you can access. You can also buy mailing lists that have been compiled from various sources.

The best lists are made up of people who subscribe to journals or other periodicals. The worst lists are made up of people who have attended trade shows or conventions.

After you create a mailing list, maintaining it is extremely important in cutting out waste and saving money. At least once or twice a year, go through the list and update it. Use the sources available in your organization to add and delete names and to correct addresses. The USPS can also help you. Ask the officials at your local post office about including "Address Correction Requested" on your self-mailing label and about the National Change of Address (NCOA) system.

ADDRESS LABELS.   Address labels must conform to USPS regulations that specify size, position, color, indicia, return address, and bar codes.

The USPS reads and sorts addresses by optical character recognition (OCR) equipment. To make your address labels conform:

- ○ Be sure the ink is dark enough.
- ○ Position the address so that it is aligned with the edges of the paper.
- ○ Use a standard typeface.
- ○ Have ample space between letters, words, and lines.
- ○ Put city, state, and zip code on the last line.
- ○ Use the standard two-letter abbreviations for states.

MAIL CLASSIFICATIONS

You can mail your newsletter either first class, second class, or third class (bulk rate). To get the current costs, contact your local post office.

FIRST-CLASS MAIL.   You should mail first class if:

○ You need fast delivery (overnight locally and two to three days nationally).

○ You want to enhance an upscale image.

○ You want to bolster the idea that the information in the newsletter is urgent.

○ You want undeliverable newsletters returned to you so that you can keep your mailing list current.

Remember that weight is critical; you pay for first-class postage by the ounce. If you mail at least two hundred newsletters, you can lower these costs substantially by presorting your newsletters. You have to follow the USPS's strict regulations, of course.

SECOND-CLASS MAIL.   You can save money by using second-class mail if:

○ You issue your newsletter regularly at least four times a year.

○ You send your newsletters to readers who pay for them, either by a subscription or a membership fee.

○ You have the resources to presort the newsletters according to postal regulations.

The amount of money you can save by using second-class rather than first-class mail is substantial and you receive the same services.

THIRD-CLASS (BULK-RATE) MAIL.   You can use third-class (bulk-rate) mail if:

○ You mail out at least two hundred newsletters.

○ All of your newsletters are identical (except for address, of course).

○ You have the resources to presort and bundle the newsletters according to postal regulations.

○ You're willing to pay a yearly fee for a bulk-mail permit.

○ Delivery time isn't a critical factor (three to six days locally, and even longer nationally).

To get faster service, mail in the middle of the month and in the middle of the week.

NOT-FOR-PROFIT STATUS

If your organization is not-for-profit, you can mail your newsletters at a much lower rate. You must officially apply to the USPS for a not-for-profit status. They will ask for documentation, such as financial reports and the bylaws of your organization.

MAILING SERVICES

If you have a large readership, you might consider using a mailing service to maintain your mailing list, print labels, and mail your newsletters. Besides the commercial mailing services, organizations such as Goodwill and United Cerebral Palsy have workshops that provide mailing services. They are a little slower, but they don't cost as much as a commercial mailing service.

OTHER METHODS OF DISTRIBUTION

Most newsletters are sent through the mail, but you can also get them to your readers by one of the following methods:

- O Route them through interoffice mail.
- O Place copies on strategically located desks or countertops.
- O Hand them out at regularly scheduled meetings.
- O Stuff copies into envelopes with other outgoing mail, a practice known as *piggybacking*. Your newsletter must be lightweight and small enough to fit into the envelope.
- O Transmit them by telecommunications. Consider this method if you have to distribute your newsletter at several locations (at all of the branch offices, for instance). Transmit the basic newsletter and let the staff at the branch office print out the number of copies they require.

SUMMARY

As you can see, some research into distribution methods, especially if you're mailing your newsletter, can save you time and money. The important points in this chapter are

1. Devise a workable method for keeping your distribution list up-to-date.
2. If you decide to mail your newsletters, contact the U.S. Postal Service for information on their stringent regulations.

3. Investigate the different classes of mail, so that you can keep your distribution costs as low as possible. If you mail out two hundred or more identical newsletters that are presorted and bundled, you can use third-class (bulk-rate) mail.

4. Besides mailing your newsletters, other distribution options include interoffice mail, hand delivery in the office or at meetings, piggybacking with other outgoing mail, and transmitting by telecommunications to distant locations.

The latest issue of your newsletter is now in the hands of your readers. It's well planned, full of lively and interesting stories, and pleasing in appearance. It entertains and serves your readers, suits the image of your organization, and fulfills its goals. Now it's time to go back to work on the next issue. I hope you enjoy it as much as I always have.

GLOSSARY

Active verbs Verbs that are direct and forceful; the subject of the sentence takes the action.

Alley The space between columns of type.

Analogy An extended metaphor, in which the writer turns an object or action into something else so that readers can see it differently or see certain elements of it more vividly.

Body In writing, the main part of a story following the lead and containing the details, clarification, documentation, and authority.

Body copy In print production, the main part of a story, set in text-style type.

Bracketing In photography, the practice of shooting at several different camera settings to ensure getting at least one good photo.

Camera-ready The copy is ready or has been prepared for the printer's camera.

Captions The descriptive text that goes with a photo or other type of illustration.

Continuous-tone copy Illustrations, including black-and-white photos, that have gradations of gray tones.

Copy Everything that is to be printed, including all art, type, and photos.

Copyfitting Editing and adjusting text so that it fits the space allowed for it in the layout.

Cropping Eliminating parts of a photo to remove detail that distracts from the main theme and to improve composition.

Deck A small headline that supports the primary headline; also called a *kicker*.

Delayed lead A lead to a story made up of one or more sentences that piqué the readers' curiosity before stating the topic; sometimes called an *indirect lead*.

Italicized terms also appear within the glossary.

Direct lead   The first one or two sentences that tell the topic of the news story.

dpi   Dots per inch. A system of measuring quality of reproduction.

Dummy   An approximation of a printed piece with the right size and folds, used as a guide for layout and printing.

Epigram   A meaningful quotation that states the theme or sets the mood at the beginning of a story.

Folio   Page number.

Font   A group of type of one style and size.

Galleys   Type set in columns on glossy paper for paste-up.

Halftone   For printing purposes, a reproduction of continuous-tone copy made up of thousands of little black dots that are varied in size and density to achieve shades of gray.

Halftone negative   The film negative of the halftone used in the printing process.

Halftone positive   A glossy paper print of a halftone, often used as a guide for the printer, sometimes used for reproduction; also called a *photostat* or a *stat*.

Headline   Text set in larger or display-size type to attract attention.

Imagesetting   A phototypesetting process used in conjunction with desktop publishing technology.

Indicia   The postal permit information that replaces the stamp.

Indirect lead   One or more sentences that piqué the reader's curiosity about the subject matter before stating the topic; sometimes called a *delayed lead*.

In register   In the printing process, to accurately position the images on the paper.

Inverted pyramid   A method for organizing a story, in which paragraphs of information are arranged in descending order of importance.

Jump line   The text that tells the reader the story is continued on another page or from another page.

Justified   Type set so that left and right margins are straight.

Kerning   A method of adjusting the space between pairs of letters so that one part of one letter overhangs part of another letter.

Kicker   A small headline that supports the primary headline; also called a *deck*.

Lead   The first few sentences of a story that announce the topic.

Leading   The space between lines of type.

Line copy   Material to be printed that is black on white, including text and illustrations such as pen-and-ink drawings.

Live-matter area   The area on the page, inside the margins, taken up by text and graphics.

Mechanical   The assemblage of type and art on paste-up boards that the printer photographs; sometimes called a *paste-up*.

Metaphor   A description of an object or action that turns it into something else so that readers can see it differently or see certain elements of it more vividly.

Mug shots   Head-and-shoulder photos of individuals.

Optical character recognition (OCR)   A type of software used with a scanner that stores the text characters in ASCII format acceptable to a computer.

Page description language (PDL)   Software that gives page makeup instructions to the computer printer.

Passive verbs   In sentences with passive verbs, the subject of the sentence, rather than taking the action, is acted upon.

Paste-up   The assemblage of type and art on paste-up boards that the printer photographs; sometimes called a *mechanical*.

Photostats   A type of halftone positive—the glossy paper print of a halftone—usually used as a guide to the printer, sometimes used for printing; also called a *stat*.

Phototypesetting   Type produced by the projection of images of characters onto photosensitive film or paper.

Pica   A unit of measurement used in print production that is 12 points in length, or roughly about one-sixth of an inch.

PMT   Photomechanical transfer print, a type of halftone positive.

Point   A unit of measurement used in print production that is roughly about $1/72$ inch.

Pull   To develop film a shorter time than usual in order to reduce the contrast and make the details sharper.

Pull-quote   Text set in a type larger than the type used for the body of a story and positioned so that it highlights an intriguing phrase or point.

Push   To develop film a longer time than usual in order to get more contrast.

Readers' profile   A description of the intended readers of a publication.

Reading diagonal   The way people typically read a document, starting at the top left corner and moving to the lower right corner.

Register   In the printing process, to position the images on the paper. *In register* means that they are positioned accurately.

Resolution   The degree of fine detail a system produces, measured in dots per inch (*dpi*).

Scaling   Determining proportions in an illustration in order to reduce or enlarge it.

Scanner   A device that "reads" and digitizes text, illustrations, and photos and transforms them into computer files for storage and manipulation.

Screen   A finely cross-ruled glass plate used with a process camera to turn continuous-tone copy into a halftone made up of dots.

Self-mailer   A newsletter designed to be mailed without an envelope. It has a printed panel containing the return address, the indicia, and space for the address label.

Serifs   The little finishing strokes that adorn the corners and extremities of characters in a typeface.

Service bureaus   Shops that specialize in imagesetting.

Short   A news story that is only one or two paragraphs long.

Sidebar   A boxed aside set within a longer story.

Simile   A brief description, comparing one object to another.

Stat   A type of halftone positive—the glossy paper print of a halftone— usually used as a guide to the printer, sometimes used for printing; short for *photostat*.

Stringer   A person who is not a regular employee, but who reports news and story ideas to a newspaper, magazine, or newsletter for one particular area.

Style guide   A document listing guidelines for spelling, punctuation, using numbers, and grammar.

Subhead   A smaller headline used to subdivide the body of a story.

Sweep line   Used in the telegraphic writing style, the topic sentence that begins a news brief and is usually set off with bolding or underlining.

Template   A skeleton version of the newsletter containing fixed elements such as the nameplate.

Tombstoning   Running headlines side by side.

Tracking   A method of adjusting the space between groups of letters.

Typeface   The design of a set of characters.

Type size   The height of type, measured in points.

Type style   A style imposed on a typeface, such as italics or bold.

Velox   Another type of halftone positive that is of a high-enough quality to be used for reproduction.

RESOURCES

BOOKS

Writing and Editing

The Chicago Manual of Style, 13th ed. Chicago and London: University of Chicago Press, 1982.

Cook, Claire Kehrwald. *Line by Line: The MLA's Guide to Improving Your Writing*. Boston: Houghton Mifflin, 1985.

Ebbett, Wilma R. and Ebbett, David R. *Writer's Guide and Index to English*, 7th ed. Chicago: Scott, Foresman, 1982.

Jordan, Lewis. *The New York Times Manual of Style and Usage*. New York: Times Books, 1982.

Shaw, Harry. *Dictionary of Problem Words and Expressions*, rev. ed. New York: McGraw-Hill, 1987.

Skillin, M. and Gay, R. *Words into Type*, 3rd ed. Englewood Cliffs, NJ: Prentice-Hall, 1974.

Stein, M. L. *Getting & Writing the News*. Chicago: Longman, 1985.

Strunk, William, Jr. and White, E. B. *The Elements of Style*, 3rd ed. New York: Macmillan, 1979.

Webster's II: New Riverside Dictionary. Boston: Houghton Mifflin, 1984. An excellent full-size dictionary.

Webster's World Dictionary: Second College Edition. New York: Simon & Schuster. A good abridged dictionary.

Zinsser, William K. *On Writing Well: An Informal Guide to Writing Nonfiction*. New York: Harper & Row, 1985.

Newsletter Publishing

Beach, Mark. *Editing Your Newsletter: How to Produce an Effective Publication Using Traditional Tools and Computers*, 3rd ed. Portland, OR: Coast to Coast Books, 1988.

Hudson, Howard P. *Publishing Newsletters*, rev. ed. New York: Charles Scribner's Sons, 1988.

Hudson, Howard Penn. *Newsletter Publishing: A Guide to Techniques and Tactics.* New York: Knowledge Industry Publications, 1987.

Desktop and Word Processing Publishing

Barry, John A., Davis, Frederic E., with Egan, Todd. *Newsletter Publishing with PageMaker. IBM Edition.* Homewood, IL: Dow Jones-Irwin, 1988.

Barry, John A., Davis, Frederic E., with Egan, Todd. *Newsletter Publishing with PageMaker. Macintosh Edition.* Homewood, IL: Dow Jones-Irwin, 1988.

Ericson, Tim & Finzer, William. *Desktop Publishing with Microsoft WORD on the Macintosh.* Alameda, CA: Sybex Computer Books, 1987.

Kleper, Michael L. *The Illustrated Handbook of Desktop Publishing and Typesetting.* Blue Ridge Summit, PA: TAB Professional and Reference Books, 1987.

Lang, Kathy. *The Writer's Guide to Desktop Publishing.* Orlando, FL: Academic Press, 1987.

Lubow, Martha. *Style Sheets for Newsletters.* Thousand Oaks, CA: New Riders Publishing, 1988. Also *Newsletter Disk Set.*

Graphics, Photography, and Print Production

Beach, Mark, Shepro, Steve, and Russon, Ken. *Getting It Printed: How to Work with Printers and Graphic Art Services to Assure Quality, Stay on Schedule, and Control Costs.* Portland, OR: Coast to Coast Books, 1986.

Calder, Julian and Garrett, John. *The New 33mm Photographer's Handbook*, rev. ed. New York: Crown, 1986.

Campbell, Alastair. *The Graphic Designer's Handbook*, new rev. ed. Philadelphia: Running Press, 1988.

Lem, Dean Phillip. *Graphics Master*, 4th ed. Los Angeles: Dean Lem Associates, 1988.

Sanders, Norman, *Graphic Designer's Production Handbook.* New York: Hasting House, 1983.

White, Jan V. *Mastering Graphics.* New York and London: R. R. Bowker, 1983.

Mailing

Bodian, Nat G. *The Publisher's Direct Mail Handbook.* Philadelphia, PA: ISI Press, 1987.

Directories

Hudson's Newsletter Directory. Published annually. The Newsletter Clearinghouse, P.O. Box 311, Rhinebeck, NY 12572.

Hudson's Washington News Media Contacts Directory. Published annually. P.O. Box 311, Rhinebeck, NY 12572.

Newsletter Directory, 3rd edition. 1987. Gale Research Co., Book Tower, Detroit, MI 48226.

Oxbridge Directory of Newsletters. 1987. Oxbridge Communications, Inc., 150 Fifth Avenue, New York, NY 10011.

PERIODICALS

Editing, Design, and Production

Editorial Eye, 85 South Bragg St. #402, Alexandria, VA 22312.

Communication Briefings, 806 Westminster Blvd., Blackwood, NY 08012.

Communications Concepts, P.O. Box 1608, Springfield, VA 22151.

The Desktop, 342 East Third St., Loveland, CO 80537.

The Editor's Forum, P.O. Box 1806, Kansas City, MO 64141.

In-House Graphics, 342 East Third St., Loveland, CO 80537.

Newsletter Design, 44 West Market St., Rhinebeck, NY 12572.

Newsletter on Newsletters, 44 West Market St., Rhinebeck, NY 12572.

Ragan Report, 407 South Dearborn St., Chicago, IL 60605.

Desktop Publishing

Desktop Publishing & Office Automation. Buyer's Guide and Handbook. Computer Information Publishing Inc., 150 Fifth Ave., New York, NY 10011.

Personal Publishing. Hitchcock Publishing Company, 25W550 Geneva Rd., Wheaton, IL 60188.

Publish! PCW Communications, Inc., 501 Second St., San Francisco, CA 94107.

ORGANIZATIONS

The Newsletter Association, 1401 Wilson Blvd., Arlington, VA 22209.

The Newsletter Clearinghouse, 44 W. Market St., P.O. Box 311, Rhinebeck, NY 12572.

INDEX